There are
Angels
in My Head!

How to Recognize
and Make Sense of
the Mystical Experience

Stickman Publications, Inc.
9004 – 35th Ave. SW Ste "G"
Seattle, WA 98126

Illustrations by Kris Wilder

Cover art, design and interior layout by Kami Miller
kzmiller.com

There are Angels in My Head/ Wilder, Kris—1st ed.

Religion / Spirituality / General

Stickman Publications, Inc.

ISBN-13: 978-0692553305

ISBN-10: 0692553304

Disclaimer

Information in this book is distributed "As Is," without warranty. Nothing in this document constitutes a legal opinion nor should any of its contents be treated as such. Neither the author nor the publisher shall have any liability with respect to information contained herein. Further, neither the authors nor the publisher have any control over or assume any responsibility for websites or external resources referenced in this book.

There are
Angels
in My Head!

How to Recognize
and Make Sense of
the Mystical Experience

_____

KRIS WILDER

Contents

Foreword

Imagine your spiritual life as a journey down a road. As you go deeper into the experience, you notice that some of the familiar billboards or signposts have been removed or overgrown. Certain things are beginning to happen to you and you are unsure of how to proceed. You may be asking yourself, what might this new sensation mean? Is this the normal path for those who are having some sort of mystical experience? What should I grasp on to, what should I quickly flee from?

Most of us either do not know, or even know how to locate, a Spiritual Director with deep experience with the mystic path. Instead, we journey alone into a new realm with no reliable compass, and we often get lost. Finding this book is like finding a compass. Br. Kris has walked this path. His deep knowledge, and experience, of the mystical, and compassion and understanding of the novice mystic makes him an invaluable guide down the deeper spiritual path. This is not a book on doctrine, dogma or collection of creeds to memorize in order to impress others with knowledge. This is a practical application of your participation in a new experience. Here you will find your questions answered even before they are asked. You have found this book because you were led to it. Now, hold the compass in your hands.

Br. Rich Atkinson
Formation Director
Order of St. Francis

Acknowledgment

To those that have held the title Teacher, many stepped into the role willingly and slipped on the trappings when needed and necessary, all while aware of their place. Each of them is owed a debt, yet none would ever think to collect.

Preface

This book is a map and not the experience.

There are many books explaining how to connect with the Divine. These books will teach you how to be more present and more focused. They may offer methods to use when exploring the ineffable. None of these books are perfect. None are all-inclusive, including this work. Walking the spiritual path is not easy, so there are many road maps. As for the road maps that are good, they have altitudes of mountains, flow of rivers, etc. Think of the maps of the new world used by early explorers. At times the maps were just too abstract to offer any accessible guidance.

It is with great difficulty that people launch into the path of mystical illumination, and it is even more difficult to maintain a path that will keep one focused on their commitment and relationship with the Divine. Often, those that actually write about their experience are so enraptured, having been touched in some manner by the Divine, that they have difficulty communicating what is happening to them. Other people that have experiences may lack the ability to mechanically communicate effectively.

Regardless of the obstacle the question remains, "How do you possibly communicate the ineffable?" The combination of these two factors—being wrapped in the experience and the lack of the words—can make it difficult to understand what is trying to be expressed.

An example of this is Pierre Teilhard de Chardin, (1881-1955) , a Jesuit mystic who tackled understanding the evolution of man and man's reunification with God in his book, *The Phenomenon of Man.* Another example is Thomas 'a Kempis (1380-1471), a monk who authored *The Imitation of Christ.* Whether you're reading 'a Kempis or Teilhard de Chardin treatises, the challenges of translations from one language to another, their attempts of relating personal experiences, editorial choices, and suppression of chapters or complete manuscripts can make it difficult to access what these mystics were saying.

Imitating others is the most fundamental and natural way for us to learn as human beings. We imitate as children. We imitate as adults, to fit in with our chosen groups or organizations. At the primitive level, one reason we attempt to fit in with others is to prevent being singled out by a predator. Or to prevent us being left behind and be forced to fend for ourselves. There is safety in groups. On the social level of the human experience, we all need a semblance of community. Even the ascetics have moments of community, relating with others as they join together in worship and during meals.

Community could be argued as a necessity that draws the line, often a line between life and death. Imitation is based on observation—we watch others and then assimilate successful behaviors. This is how we learn, this is what brings structure to community and society, and imitation of what has worked for those that have come before.

When we go to church we use the successful behaviors. These behaviors allow us to fit in and eventually go deeper into the experience. When you are in doubt on what to do, the prayer book will guide you. Also those who know what to do are dressed apart from us and are easy to identify and follow. This designation could be a set of robes or they may take a physical position in the building. Regardless, the signals are clear and present, and we are able to easily fit into our chosen group.

To seek a numinous path, you may choose a group that does not necessarily possess robes or a path that doesn't necessarily have manuals based on consensus. And even when you do have written materials in hand, they may be difficult to comprehend for reasons mentioned above. All of this can make for a difficult and sometimes painful road. It is not easy. However, it is without hesitation that I tell you the rewards are abundant and profound.

This journey should always be a complement to participation in a like-minded community. These communities may or may not be mutually exclusive. For instance, on Sunday mornings, when we walk into a church, we know precisely what we are doing and we know why we are there. But this book assumes that you are walking on a path that lacks many of the mechanical attributes of physically attending a church. Even though we may have a church community that community may not necessarily serve us, in total on this path.

This mystical path is one that takes place every day and at any place, according to Brother Lawrence . In his book, *The Practice of the Presence of God,* he addressed how he changed the tedious task of going into town to fetch burgundy wine for the brothers of his monastery into a spiritual experience. Brother Lawrence's work in the kitchen became moments to connect with God.

When we open up the prayer book and follow as a group, if we get lost, we can lean over and glance at the page number of the parishioner next to us. Often on the mystical path you will find yourself in experiences, where there is no parishioner next to you that you can nudge and ask for a page number.

This is a matter that must be made as clear as possible. The day you suspect that you have outgrown the experience of communal worship, you have lost your way. Not in the sense that you have moved into a new experience, but that you placing one below the other. Simply put, seeking a solitary path can be an act of ego and should be scrutinized. Even the most ascetic of Christians, whether St. Anthony of the Desert or the modern monks of the Chartreuse monastery, have community and discussion. In its smallest forms, community provides the tether to keep you present in this life.

The majority of your friends, relatives, and even spouses will not fully understand the path in which you are engaged. This lack of understanding is completely normal. Some of what you are doing and experiencing will not be appreciated or even validated.

This experience is difficult to appreciate, and I would contend it might never be understood by the mind, yet the heart understands it. Anything that is difficult to understand, or may seem threatening, has the tendency be placed by the observer into an environment where fear can raise its head. This can be a fear towards what you do and and what you experience. That fear, in turn, will be labeled. Such labeling can be savage. You can and will be accused of not being a true Christian, worshiping Satan, not praying properly, or having misplaced priorities. If these labels seem harsh, or you have not experienced them yet, rest assured that these and other trials are coming your way.

It is with these cautionary comments that I urge you to stay anchored within your faith, trust those who have come before you, know that you are not alone in that

Christ is always with you, God is always with you, and the Holy Spirit is always with you.

As you've probably already discovered, you're beginning to move your thought process from a zero sum thought process to having, as an example, more compassion. You may also be experiencing your joys and successes in ways that are more emotionally real than in the past. In other words, your connections with your fellow man are not just of the human experience. You're binding the human experience and the soul, creating a more global experience than one of superficial clichés.

The shifting of attitudes, perspectives, and qualities of life that you are experiencing are inward movements, and at the same time as outward movements. The inward movement is usually the first in the sequence of these experiences. An example might be the embracing of retreating from some of the things that you used to do that brought you a sense of fun like a child that no longer finds their once favorite cartoon engaging anymore. This is often followed by the outward. This could be described as maybe the desire to replace the cartoons with a desire for documentaries and then both simultaneously. The ability to see the deeper humor of the cartoon and also the power of a historical event on which the cartoon is making fun. God is not bound to endow these experiences on you in this order—this is just the most common initial experience. What you probably discovered at this point is down is up and up is down.

The things that are of value to God, Christ and the Holy Spirit are sometimes the least valued by the human experience as a collective. And yet you found that in engaging in these moments you've found your greatest joy. This is because your values are beginning to align with higher levels of awareness. This is a joyous, exciting, and vibrant time.

As this experience of alignment unfolds, don't be tempted to look ahead, to peek around the corner to see what God has in store. Frankly, nobody knows what God has planned for any of us. Enjoy your experience and prepare for the future, but don't try to make the future conform to your will. Only a fool has the boldness to tell God what you expect from him.

All seekers of the mystical experience are drawn like the proverbial moth to a flame. This overused metaphor is too appropriate to pass over here. A moth cannot possibly comprehend the light that it seeks, yet it does seek the light. The moth can't possibly comprehend even why it seeks the light. The moth cannot truly access the totality of the light. If the moth were successful in its goal of passing through the glass barrier of the light bulb and making it to the core of the light bulb, the white-hot filament, its physicality would cease.

Conformity is a human experience probably best exemplified by the teenage experience. At the teenage stage of life, it's important for them to conform to the drives, wants and wishes of their peer group. However, they still want to be seen as individuals. This is a very difficult time in life because teens have two divergent powers pulling at their sense of self. One power demands conformity, and if rules aren't followed, the teenager will be mocked, abused, and even ostracized from the clique. On the other side of this experience, the teenager is busy trying to separate themselves from the family in many ways including listening to different music than their parents and avoiding being seen with their parents. Family gatherings and church events are two familiar institutions that most teenagers attempt to avoid.

The contemporary seeker is familiar with the experience of grappling with the opposing desires of the need to conform and the need for individuality. When you began to experience God in a unique and personal way, a way that differs from your peer group, you will be tested – by parishioners, family members, and friends.

This "testing" experience comes in two simple forms. The first is questioning. The questioner may be attempting to seek understanding and appreciation of your experience. Or, the questioning may be designed to find flaws in your experience so that you can be called back in accord with the group with which you originated. The interest that a person takes in your journey, along with the line of questioning, reveals their path quickly. These two lines of attention can be described as interest or compliance.

The second form is ignoring what you are doing. Because someone cannot comprehend or participate in a conversation about religious experience, they decide to avoid addressing what is happening in and around you, altogether. This may be caused by a fear of the unknown, a fear of their experience or a fear of what your experience may be. As odd as it may sound, many fear the illumination that the Holy Spirit can bring to their life.

In all of these instances, you must accept the position of others, assuming that they have not struck an extreme position where someone is being harmed. Sometimes this is frustrating, but it is the best path to choose. Keep in mind that when you allow others to have their experience, you must keep on guard so that the integrity of your own experience remains intact.

A primary challenge the modern seeker faces is how the mystical experience breaks free of the religiosity of their institution and yet still remains attached. St. Francis lived in a time before clocks. In one event he turned to his traveling companions and announced it was time for prayer and without a clock to tell them the precise time and no prayer books to guide them they stopped their travel and sat in prayer. This may seem like an odd configuration, but look at it this way: the first aspect of the experience is to have the internal tools for the disciplines needed to navigate the experience. Disciplines are essential for order. Without order, there can be no continuity of experience. Order and anchoring is what the Church and the associated doctrine bring to the mystical experience. Every major religion has an order and structure brought forth by centuries of experience. To throw these institutions aside as useless and cumbersome is an act of hubris.

In sum, in the same way that your personal experience is simultaneously inward and outward, you can have an experience that is simultaneously religious and mystical. The essential nature of the interplay between the religious and the mystical is the subject of the following chapters.

Introduction

"A good traveler has no fixed plans and is not intent on arriving."

                                    - Lao Tzu[5]

The structure of this book involves surveying the mystical landscape before construction begins. Part of this survey involves some historical background. The beginning lays out a metaphor that will be used throughout this book, followed by a summary of the historical structure of this book. Some time is spent on the structure of the brain. It is important to have an overview of the functions and methods of the brain as these functions and methods are the filters, receiver and sometimes the deceiver of the mystical experience. The majority of this book is a breakdown of various types of experiences, the reason is to allow for a well stocked tool box as the experiences manifest, and to aid in recognition and assessment where necessary.

What you will find in this book is a map. What you will not find are action items at the end of each chapter, or boxes to check off. That part is for you to do on your own. You have to live into and be responsible for your experience.

You will also not find guidance about how to discern the mystical experience, to understand what is happening to you or how to deal with a particular experience, either. Grappling with the experience is the realm of spiritual directors, priests, and elders. This book is not designed to explain an experience in hard and fast rules but to present the exterior, the container, and the attributes of a moment.

Look at this book as if it is a road map. Roads tell you where you are. The road is an assured path laid by others that know the way. However, there are different types of roads. Roads are classified as federal, state, county, city, private, and others that are not labeled. The federal road is an interstate, with many lanes, barriers, and clear lines to separate the lanes. State roads are the purview of the state government. The quality and style of state roads are often driven by financing and not necessarily by use and importance. The next level of road is the county road—it has only two lanes, each going in the opposite direction. The side of the road might have guardrails at some identified dangerous points, and soft shoulders, used only for emergencies to get out of the main traffic flow.

During wintertime, maintenance crews clear city streets of snow at a city's expense. Curbs and parking are also the responsibility of the city. In older cities, these roads are based on human and animal paths carved out over hundreds of years. Private roads are often marked with a "Private Road" sign. They may lead to a dead end or to somebody's private property marked "No Trespassing."

Each road is a different experience. An interstate might allow high speeds, while and at the other end of spectrum the one marked "Private Road" might require a four-wheel-drive vehicle.

There are many people, and books, that will tell you how to have a mystical experience. These books might suggest a certain hand position or minimum time durations in physical or mental states. Many are valid, and some are not. This book doesn't directly address the validity of methods, but it does address determining validity via testing. By breaking down the mystical experience into categories and qualities, you will learn to see the experience as meaningful and valid, or as an obfuscation of the truth. And there is a difference.

An example is the contrast between a rollercoaster and a car—you can experience a wonderful stomach-dropping ride on a roller coaster, and you can get a similar sensation in a fast car on a hilly road. One is controlled and safe, while the other is less controlled and is riskier. The sensation in the car is real, but danger is high as you careen over hilly roads exceeding the speed limit. But at the end of the joyride, you find yourself in a new location, whereas the rollercoaster takes you back to the beginning. Both sensations are similar, but one is dangerous and the other is safe. One moves you to a new land, and one is just a thrill. This is not to say that the spiritual path is dangerous, but surely, it can be perilous.

All the world's religions have spiritual leaders, and many have attested to the rough experiences that they encountered. The temptation of Jesus by the devil, the attack of Mara the Tempter upon Buddha under the Bo tree, or the night attacks on Padre Pio by demonic forces, are just three examples of such events.

Millarium

The destination was Vindolanda, an outpost on Hadrian's Wall. Hadrian's Wall, begun in 122 A.D., separated northern England from Scotland. As we neared our destination, I noticed a few stone monoliths along the road. Pointing one out I asked my host, "What are those?" He replied, "Those are Roman road signs. They are Millarium."

The Millarium was the word Romans used for their milestones. A carved stone was placed every mile along a Roman road. The Millarium was used to reassure travelers that they were on the correct path. As the Roman Empire expanded into territories unknown or unfamiliar, the milestone was a well-received demarcation by the traveler. The milestone was a validation from a higher source and an indication that others of your kind had traveled this road before.

How would you, as a traveler, use the Millarium? Imagine this: You leave Rome and head out over land to your outpost at Hadrian's Wall. You leave in the spring, crossing the Alps, crossing the vast fields in Gaul (what is modern day France), and possibly marching through part of what is now Belgium. You cross the English Channel by ship and continue north, over land, across England to your final destination of Hadrian's Wall.

1

The farther you travel from Rome, the less you hear your native tongue; the more unusual the customs, and the more unfamiliar the foods, become. Soon, the Millarium, with the name of your Emperor in your native tongue, provide a rare kernel of familiarity. These milestones demonstrate you are on the right path, regardless of your confusion, real and perceived threats, and new experiences.

My hope is that this book will serve as a road map with a few Millarium posted on the way for a journey to connect with the God, The Creator, and to experience Unio Mystica, the final stage of the spiritual path in the Christian spiritual tradition. This book helps you to embark on this journey, or to continue on this journey, even without including a treatise on methods. Such methods vary widely, and though many are valid, none are paths to all Truth.

A Pentecostal gathering, with its fervor and physical experience of the divine, is as valid as a group of Protestants standing up and reciting a statement of faith together. If you're seeking the magic hand position, this book does not include the symbol or methods of verbalization to ensure the Most High hears your prayers. There are aids to the journey, but there are few secret keys, outside of dedication and application. The assumption is that you already have a path that you follow, and experiences to account on that path

You won't find a lot of biblical quotes or constant references that travel down the rabbit hole of The Greek, Latin, Hebrew, and Aramaic in this book, either. They are all important but only used when necessary. Dropping in and out scripture, dissecting origin and use of words, and contextualizing via history is important. However, I am not a linguistics expert, nor a biblical historian. Such matters are better left to those that make deep and responsible studies of them. I am only a Brother that has been trained and have a level of involvement in these matters. Although this book has certain textbook attributes, these types of references are used sparingly.

This is not an effort to unlink terms from their place in history or lose their root meaning, but an effort to create a document that is easy to read. For instance, statements like, "In the Greek, meaning to love." are used lightly. This type of annotation is available in many manuscripts and, dear reader, you are encouraged to seek out the background and roots of words for further study.

Rewards

The path of mystical Christianity is not one that is full of material rewards. The rewards are impossible to describe and impossible to touch. The mystical Christian path appears to be a course of foolishness to many people. The mystical path turns the material world upside down. It does not make any promises about how to have a perfect family, or how to make an income you deserve, or how to manifest wealth, love, or how to bring understanding to your life. We have all heard the phrase "world turned upside down" before, usually in the context of a personal crisis. It usually conveys that the experience is bad, and is not the one that they expected or sought out. Your inversion experience, on the other hand, is not always one of suffering or terror. Instead, it is a willful experience. It is an engagement of your choosing, a deliberate relenting of your ego that slips you into a relationship with the Divine.

In fact, the Christian mystical path can only assure you that it will make demands that will be difficult for you to fulfill. It will make demands on your body, mind, brain, and spirit.

Christian mysticism will test your religion, and it will test your spirituality. It will take you to places that you want to go, as well as places that you do not want to go. You will see things that will inspire, and you will also see things that are frightful. More importantly you will see yourself in an all-loving and illuminating light of God.

The external trappings that you may have with regard to a religious or spiritual commitment, like a robe or cincture, a title, or a position, are nice but not necessary. The reference is of the internal commitment that begins right where you are and then faithfully steps forward into the experience. The word "faithfully" is specifically chosen over the word "intelligently" because God is worthy of your heart and your mind and not only your capacity to acquire and apply knowledge.

Giovanni Battista Scaramelli

"Those who know nothing of foreign languages know nothing of their own."

- *Johann Wolfgang von Goethe*[6]

The codifications of the mystical experience in this book are based on the works of G.B. Scaramelli (1687-1752). A great debt is owed to him in his structure, clarity, and solid foundation.

Giovanni Battista Scaramelli is not a common household name, nor is it a name that is usually brought up in the world of the mystical experience. Some might say that Scaramelli's work is uninventive, mundane, and unexciting. But his work is anything but. Scaramelli outlines and offers us a roadmap to the mystical experience that is rare for the Western world. This is how his work is inventive—he put it to paper. The exploration of the mystical is not mundane in the least, and for that matter, it is hardly unexciting.

His source work can be found in *Il Directtorio Mistico,* published in Italy in 1754. The Il Directtorio Mistico, was published in English for the first time, 169 years later (1923), in London, by John Watkins. The most recent published digest is *A Handbook of Mystical Theology,* Scaramelli, 2005. Translated by D.H.S Nicolson, Introduction by Allan

Armstrong. Berwick, Maine Ibis Press, an imprint of Nicolas-Hays, Inc., 2005.

Giovanni Battista Scaramelli was born in Rome in 1687 and died 65 years later in January of 1752. A 19-year-old Giovanni entered the Catholic order of The Society of Jesus, commonly referred to as the Jesuits. It is not known the terms in which the 19-year-old Giovanni entered the Society of Jesus, but it wouldn't be too much of a leap to assume that this was his heart's desire as opposed to the need for food and warmth. It is also likely that by the age of 19 he may have already learned reading and writing, and he possibly came from an above-average family in the socioeconomic strata of the day. It is unlikely that he had anything else but a Catholic upbringing, being born to the faith and not a convert. This would also aid him in the admission into the order at nineteen years of age. What is known and surmised about Scaramelli is this we can draw a very succinct line from admission to the order, taking vows in the order of the Society of Jesus and eventually becoming a priest. As for his day-to-day activities, those would be structured.

Scaramelli's *A Handbook of Mystical Theology* is just that—a handbook designed to be used, studied and digested by aspirants seeking a deeper mystical experience.

Scaramelli Schematic

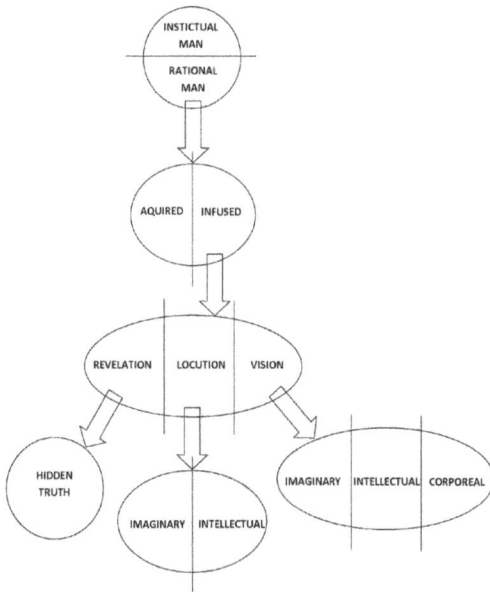

The Brain, the Mind and Knowing the Difference

"Brain: an apparatus with which we think we think."

- Ambrose Bierce[7]

The brain being one of the filters with which we experience the world also serves the same purpose for experiencing the mystical. Having an overview of how the brain interacts with the mystical experience is necessary to aid in telling the difference between truth and falsehood. Further much of the brain in hardwired.

Some people are predisposed to alcoholism; it is a genetic trait that sits in their brain. Some people have seizures when certain combinations of lights flash rapidly, as in some video games. And some predispositions are less obvious and are of little consequence to the outside world.

Once, as I sat at the breakfast table, I watched my four-year-old son point to the color green and call it orange. I recall the moment in first grade that I observed myself transposing green for orange and vice versa. Soon I had developed a little protocol to prevent the transposition from happening, or at least preventing the verbalization of this transposition. I've spent my life deliberately switching the words and colors from the mental mix-up to make the correct word go with the correct color when I wish to speak of colors. If given no attention, I am likely to call orange, green and green, orange even while understanding and recognizing that the name mix-up has taken place. So my son calling the color green, orange appeared to be genetic. Some behaviors are innate and inescapable, and today locatable to specific regions of the brain. The brain can deceive you, it can switch a color and its name, or it can kill you, in the case of chronic alcoholism.

The brain is the center of the human neurological system. Anatomically, the brain is composed of several sections. The brainstem, which connects to the spinal cord, is where you find basic functions such as respiration and pulse. The cerebellum deals with balance and mobility. The right and left hemispheres of the brain, the cerebrum, control functions like memory, vision, and speaking.

The frontal lobes are where conscious thought, voluntary movement, and personality originate. The occipital lobes are in the back of the brain—colors and visual space are interpreted in this part of the brain. Temporal lobe functions include memory and hearing, while the cerebral cortex covers the cerebrum. Deep inside the human brain is the corpus callosum. The corpus callosum is a super neurological highway that connects the left cerebral cortex to the right cerebral cortex to allow information and thought to flow between the two hemispheres of the brain.

Human Brain

The Corpus Callosum

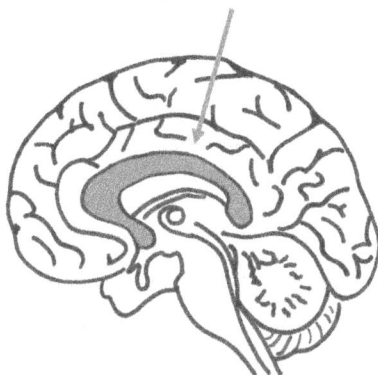

One popular way to look at brain processes is in an ascending hierarchical fashion. These three levels are the lizard brain, the monkey brain, and the human brain.

The lizard brain functions on four simple protocols. When a creature (such as a human) encounters something bigger than itself, the brain's protocol is to run away. If the other creature is the same size, the protocol is to stay and fight it, or possibly even have sex with it. If what is being confronted is smaller, the protocol is to eat it.

13

Human Brain

Lizard Brain or Reptilian Brain

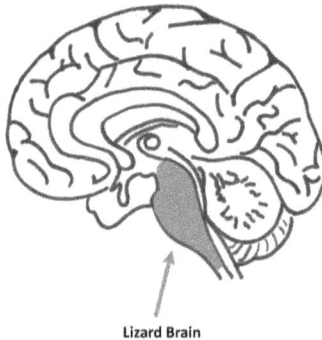

Lizard Brain

The monkey brain, uses these three aspects of the lizard brain, and then adds social functionality, such as tribe behavior, or extended care for offspring.

Human Brain

Monkey Brain or Limbic System

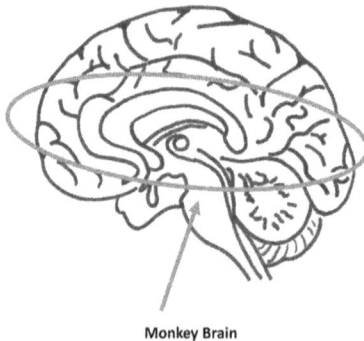

Monkey Brain

The human brain (cerebral cortex) allows us to discuss displaced phenomena, use tools, travel outside our own environments, and engage in complex strategic planning.

But these experiences are not expressed in hard and fast lines. For example, some apes can use sign language, can express emotions, and refer to items not seen.

Human Brain

Cerebral Cortex

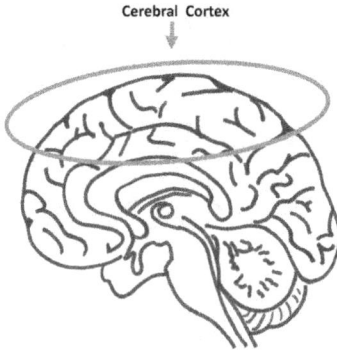

The Prefrontal Cortex v. The Amygdala

The Amygdala contains the lizard brain, the fight or flight response, and the base functions of existence.

Human Brain

The Amygdala

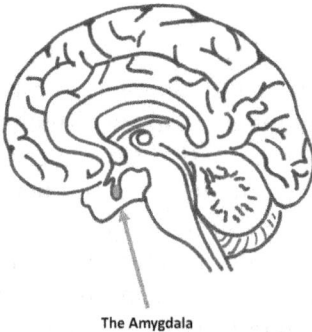

The prefrontal cortex is the executive part of the brain. This executive controls social activity, suppresses urges, and helps make decisions based on prediction.

Human Brain

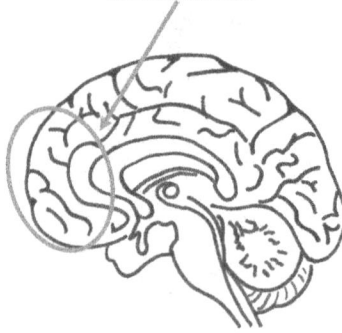

The corpus callosum is the neurological highway between the left and right brain.

The corpus callosum constricts during a stressful situation, restricting the flow of communication between the artistic side of the brain and the logical side of the brain.

This restriction of the corpus callosum allows the amygdala to take control of the body's reaction to a stress situation. Think of it this way: the amygdala is pushing the other parts of the brain aside while saying, "You don't know what you're doing! Get out of the way!" With a simple set of rules to guide itself, the amygdala always knows what it is going to do in any situation, fight or flight, with the introduction of the adrenal dump, a term used in combat and sports to describe the chemical cocktail the body uses to increase strength and speed as an example. With the adrenal dump, time also becomes distorted, tunnel vision takes over, hearing is impaired, and blood flow patterns change to meet the physical needs to deal with the stress. Detachment from one's emotions can also occur.

The higher the stress level in your life, the less your brain communicates with itself and the more this lizard brain, with its four simple rules of survival, controls your existence. Even the kind of ambient stress of a morning commute to work can put the amygdala in control.

Clearly, life without stress is impossible. Even monks in monasteries experience stress. Stress always finds its way into your life as part of the human condition. Learning to manage the stress removes the amygdala from taking a role, thus allowing the brain to function at a higher level.

The Brain and Change

"To improve is to change; to be perfect is to change often."
                                    - *-Winston Churchill*[3]

Mike is an old acquaintance and a gifted classical guitarist. As I sat in his studio and listened to him play, it was clear why he was on staff at a local university teaching guitar. I was curious how he became so accomplished, and Mike revealed some of his techniques that improved his performance. The little things, like focusing on the middle phalanx of his third finger or ring finger to create the correct pressure, were part of his routine. He practiced repetitive drills and then deliberately scrambled them up to challenge the imprint he had created. Certainly, Mike was training his fingers and hands, but the greatest change was taking place in his brain.

The brain is plastic, it changes. Examples such as the neurological rewiring, of the brain with Alzheimer's disease, and changes that take place in the brain during adolescence, are confirmation of the brain's ability to rewire itself without your attention. The form of neuroplasticity that interests us is not the automatic rewiring triggered by time and hormones, but an active, deliberate retooling of the brain. It's about shaping the brain, in the same way that Mike did to improve his classical guitar performance.

Some studies in this brain-retooling field are found in the works of Gaser and Schlaug (Christian Gaser, 8 October 2003). They concluded that musicians have areas of the brain that are more highly developed than those of the average non-musician.

In regard to retooling the brain for a deeper and significant mystical experience, Dr. Andrew Newberg, MD explored the brain during prayer. He found that certain parts of the brain became more active (Dr. Andrew Newberg, 2010). Additional researchers are scanning the brains of Buddhist monks to observe the effects of mindfulness on the reshaping of the brain.

The old adage holds true: The brain *is* like a muscle. Studies show that the brain is plastic and will develop and build areas that are needed for certain tasks. Prayer and meditation exercise reshape the brain. These prayer and meditation exercises are like the scales of the classical guitar—they are the tools that allow you hear the music of the Divine.

Rhythm

People love rhythm. They like consistency. Contrary to what people say about liking or needing change, they prefer incremental change to large-scale change. Ask the person that is using drugs if they want to change and the answer is "No." Only after users have hit their lowest point, often called hitting "rock bottom," are they willing to change. They make this choice because they finally understand that they may lose their life. Sadly this kind of story is familiar with many of us.

When it comes to change, it is easy to do when the social cost is low. It is easier to leave Catholicism and become a Lutheran, because you need just drop a few manuscripts and streamline the ritual of the religious service. Clearly this is a simplification of the details, yet the concept is that there is not that big of a leap to make this change. However, dropping the Catholic version of Christianity for Buddhism is a colossal leap and very expensive in social and emotional ways. By exchanging Christianity for Buddhism, You are leaving one spiritual world that is based on advocacy salvation for another spiritual world based on enlightenment salvation.

Of course, such a socially, and emotionally expensive journey is not often undertaken. It is much easier to seek the simple addition or deletion of a manuscript or ritual. The essential tenets of the religion remain the same. Only the edges of the religion change. In the same way, it is easier to paint your house to make a change than it is to seek change by selling your house, buying a new one, and moving on.

So when a higher spiritual existence is sought, it can be just as difficult as changing from being a Catholic to becoming a Buddhist. This is not about Christ or the Buddha. It's about how extreme yet similar the path can be. And that extreme growth or change does not happen around the edges—it happens at the core and the rhythm changes.

The Mind

*"Cancer can take away all of my physical abilities.
It cannot touch my mind, it cannot touch my heart, and
it cannot touch my soul."*

- *Jim Valvano*[9]

When my grandfather died, my family gathered for the service to be held in our small hometown. People traveled from all over to pay their respects and honor his life. His wife, my grandmother, was deep into the dance of Alzheimer's. At this point in her life, names of friends, relatives, and children escaped her. She recently decided she was going to walk to Germany, and from the West Coast of the United States, it is of course impossible. This once intelligent church organist, who played cards as if it were a contact sport, was not present anymore. During her husband's funeral she said nothing, was cordial as it was the right thing to do, and was treated gently by the mourners as they understood her condition. After the service, the family gathered at the home with a few close family friends. Grandma said nothing, her mind would not let her. As the post service meal was readied, she sat at the head of a long oak table lined with her children, grandchildren, and in-laws. As the plates were filled and people were settled, she spoke, unannounced:

"I would like to thank all of you." All the hustle of the moment was stilled, she paused for a moment as if to gather her thoughts, and then continued. Grandma spoke in brief and thoughtful sentences, she acknowledged everybody's effort, the appreciation she had for everyone and for making the day a very good day.

Then she stopped speaking and returned to her life as it had become. For a moment, Grandma was back. How did it happen? How did grandma, for a brief moment, transform back into the woman that we all knew? Her brain was no longer capable of that kind of process. It is my belief, unscientific and based on a desire to have her back, that it was her essence speaking, and not her brain, for a just a moment.

The argument is this: Are the mind and the brain two different things? Is our sense of self housed in the brain or does our sense of self live outside of the brain? An aid to understanding the mystical experiences starts with agreeing with both Socrates and Plato that the mind is separate from the body.

The soul is conscious. The soul is part of the human body in as much as the soul interacts with the body but is not of the body. When the body dies, the soul, the consciousness, lives on. Theologians and philosophers have argued about this brain/mind issue since before the idea was recorded on paper.

It is not important to argue or parse the ideas. Is the soul the mind? Is the brain the mind? It makes little difference to the person experiencing the Divine. But it is helpful to know how to tune the mechanical brain so that it may receive inspiration from the Divine. This is why it is important to understand the basic idea that the brain, and certain parts of the brain, can dominate an experience.

The effort of the ego trying to burst forward, and seize control of your thoughts is important to recognize as well, because the ego will use the brain to suit its needs. It is as if your brain is a gas-powered lawn mower. Under the right operator, it will create a beautiful lawn. With no operator, the mower will do its job of mowing without discriminating between flower and grass.

A Quick and Incomplete Overview of Trying to Touch the Divine

This is not a section on methods or the validity of certain types of meditations over another. Nor will the purposes or goals of certain techniques be addressed. There are hard, fast rules, and then there are less rigid boundaries. And within these items are subsets, a complex set of theories and methods that are covered in volumes of works by others and spanning the known history of man. They all aspire to the larger direction of enlightenment and perfection.

Meditations can be seen as forms of mental and spiritual attunement. These forms can cross over from one into another. The methods and techniques used are left to you as you seek your own spiritual direction.

Meditation

Meditation is the active training of the mind to bring about a change in the conscious level of the practitioner. It's a proven method of regulating the mind and body. The goal can be to relax or develop a state of being. Practices and methods can vary, ranging from the time of day a person engages in meditation to the number of beads on a string.

Contemplation

"Contemplation" is derived from the Latin word *contemplatio*. Contemplation differs from meditation. In meditation, there is one point of focus, say the breath, or candlelight, and clarity of mind is sought. In contemplation, the process involves pondering of the attributes of an object, person, or idea. There is a noun, a person, place or thing at the center of the mental activity.

Prayer

Prayer is the deliberate act of communication with a deity. The initiator of the prayer is trying to develop a connection with God as they know God to be.

The Four Phases of Life

"Turn! Turn! Turn!"
To everything - turn, turn, turn
There is a season - turn, turn, turn
And a time to every purpose under heaven

A time to be born, a time to die
A time to plant, a time to reap
A time to kill, a time to heal
A time to laugh, a time to weep

To everything - turn, turn, turn
There is a season - turn, turn, turn
And a time to every purpose under heaven

A time to build up, a time to break down
A time to dance, a time to mourn
A time to cast away stones
A time to gather stones together

To everything - turn, turn, turn
There is a season - turn, turn, turn
And a time to every purpose under heaven

A time of love, a time of hate
A time of war, a time of peace
A time you may embrace
A time to refrain from embracing

To everything - turn, turn, turn
There is a season - turn, turn, turn
And a time to every purpose under heaven

A time to gain, a time to lose
A time to rend, a time to sew
A time for love, a time for hate
A time for peace, I swear it's not too late!

- *#1 on the Hot 100 chart on December 4, The Byrds*[10] *1965*

A Native American woman spoke about her tribe in a classroom setting. She talked about many aspects of tribal life, including family relationships, leaders and subordinates, adults and children. She pointed out how her tribal council works. She said, "When you're thirty, you can come to the meetings and listen, when you're forty, you can come to the meetings and listen and speak. When you're fifty, you can come to the meetings and you can listen, speak and vote."

This window into this woman's tribal methods demonstrated an innate understanding of the four phases of life.

The famous psychologist Carl Jung wrote a book called, *Modern Man in Search of a Soul* (Jung, 1955). In this book, he discussed the four stages of life. The following section is based on Carl Jung's work on these life phases.

These phases are similar to the four seasons: spring, summer, fall and winter. It's a familiar cycle in East Indian culture where a man throws away all the things that he owns during the winter of his life and becomes a Sannyasa Ashrama, a renunciant.

Carl Jung's work on the four phases of life is not just insightful. It can be observed in human existence. How do these four phases of life apply to the Christian mystical experience?

Phase 1. The Athlete
Phase 2. The Warrior
Phase 3. The Statesman
Phase 4. The Priest(ess)

These are not direct translations of Carl Jung's four phases, but they are modified here to speak to the Christian mystical experience.

The Athlete

The 1988 baseball movie *Bull Durham* centers on a minor league baseball team from Durham, North Carolina. Crash Davis, the older catcher who is on the downside of his baseball career, helps teach the wild and youthful pitcher Ebby Calvin LaLoosh after watching LaLoosh's bad interview post an impressive win. Sitting on the team bus Crash Davis takes ahold of LaLoosh and explains to him that his post game interview was not good, that the athlete self failed to communicate to the rest of the people, the fans listening, in a way they could get it.

> *Crash Davis: "…it's time to work on your interviews."*
>
> *Ebby Calvin LaLoosh: "My interviews? What do I gotta do?"*
>
> *Crash Davis: "You're gonna have to learn your clichés. You're gonna have to study them. You're gonna have to know them. They're your friends. Write this down: We gotta play 'em one day at a time."*
>
> *Ebby Calvin LaLoosh: "Got to play…(pauses and looks up at Davis) it's pretty boring."*
>
> *Crash Davis: "'Course it's boring, that's the point. Write it down. I'm just happy to be here and hope I can help the ballclub." (LaLoosh pauses again, looks at Davis) "I know, write it down. I just wanna give it my best shot and the good Lord willing, things will work out."*

- -   *The Movie Bull Durham*[11]

Davis is teaching LaLoosh how to control his Athlete and to ape a more mature version of himself until he can grow into his skills.

This is the phase of life where the primary sense of self is derived from the physical body. It is based on how you look, the physical shape of your body, your health, what kind of clothes you wear, and what kind of car you drive. It can be termed a materialistic existence. Teenagers are an excellent example of this phase of life.

Young professional athletes often exemplify this phase of life and are easily observable because of their public profile. Often, these athletes are more concerned about the kind of car they drive and how much gold they wear instead of the performance of their team. Sometimes these players take this to such an extreme degree that they are considered to be selfish and non-cooperative. They place their own sense of accomplishment and wellbeing so far beyond that of a team or organization that they become a grotesque distortion of this phase of life.

The positive aspect of this phase of life, of course, is the vitality and resilience of the body. It can heal quickly and work strongly. The body is at the apex of its performance. It has never been this strong before, and in the future will never achieve at this level again.

The Warrior

Donald Trump is explaining a lateral move, the vacating of a failed project for a more productive project. The volume of money may be more, and that means success in the warrior world.

This time of life is about acquisition. It is about acquiring a spouse and a home as opposed to the Athlete State, which is about accessing resources and making comparisons to others. At this stage of life, it is important to have jet skis in tow behind the SUV you own. This phase it is about vacationing at the best places, having the right clothes, and being seen with the right people. This is not to say that people in this stage are the extreme caricatures presented for our purposes, each phase contains elements of the other. It is quite possible to have two jet skis and volunteer at the local homeless shelter.

Similar to the athlete, the focus is still on the body, but this focus is more sophisticated. Long-term goals are now more important, so delayed gratification is acceptable.

The Statesman

"The best way to find yourself is to lose yourself in the service of others."

               - *Mahatma Gandhi*[13]

At the end of a newscast you will find the "happy kicker", a story that is about the positive humanity of man. The goal of the story is to leave you with a warm fuzzy feeling about the program. Upon examination, the stories are often about people helping others, such as a group cleaning a creek filled with debris, helping to complete a park project, walking for a cure for cancer. People that are in their mature years of life organize the majority of these events. When kids, or young adults organize these sorts of events, it sounds like a "Man bites dog" story, seeming reversed and odd.

This Statesman phase of life is when one begins to turn back towards their community, the environment in which they live. Some examples of this are a desire to become a member of the school board, a church leader, and, donating to a community activity or organizational goal.

The cornerstone of this phase is placing the goals of the organization above their own immediate needs. Their life and actions are not necessarily about servicing the pressing demands of the self. They are about addressing the long-term goals of their family and community to bring bounty to others in forms that they can use or need.

The Priest(ess)

"It is the preoccupation with possessions, more than anything else that prevents us from living freely and nobly."

- Bertrand Russell [14]

This is the place in life when personal values have completely shifted from the material to the relational. Relationships with one's neighbors, friends, and family and to one's God have a far greater value than the clothes that a person wears or the car that they drive.

Often, the ego becomes smaller, and with this resizing of self, the values shift. The person takes on a new phase of life. Sometimes they physically change in an almost caterpillar-to-butterfly transformation. They often act differently, more metered, more circumspect and less likely to rush to judgment. They have a deeper commitment to God that takes on features that are different than that of the commitment from the Athlete, the Warrior, or the Statesman. The Priest's commitment is one of internalization, a knowing, and a desire for attachment with the limitless and eternal God, all marked by contemplation.

It is difficult to follow a Christian mystic path at a young age. The Athlete and the Warrior are inclined to adopt a preformed shape of God that fits their egos.

45

Examples of breaking away from the bindings of life can be illustrated by the ascetic life, one of severe self-discipline and removal from all forms of indulgence. Asceticism is practiced by the desert fathers, or to some degree, the monastic forms of many religious orders. Possessing several attributes of this life in different degrees, you could also point to the simple life exemplified by the Quakers.

These regimes remove items from life that might feed the deep desires of the early stages of life. These desires can be detrimental to a fully actualized life. A simple life removed of fast cars, modern music, and media leave time for contemplation and do not feed the youthful needs of acquisition in a high-velocity way.

The religious path, which in most cases is a necessary precursor to the mystical path, is well suited for youth. It provides the foundation upon which further stages of growth are based.

Behaving inappropriately for a time in life can become a ridiculous caricature. It is as if a grandmother decided to adopt the dress styles of her teenage granddaughter. It would not only be considered inappropriate, it would also be seen as a very poor decision, calling into question her mental stability. If you reversed these roles, with the granddaughter adopting the dress and manners of her grandmother, the granddaughter's behavior would be considered odd, maybe quirky and clearly outside the norm, but not necessarily disturbing.

It is the same with the religious experience, and with the mystical experience. Take the measure of your space and place. Understand your role and participation as much as possible, and then set an open course toward growth from the point where you are to the unseen horizon.

There Is One Best Way

> *"Not every difficult and dangerous thing is suitable for training, but only that which is conducive to success in achieving the object of our effort."*
>
> - *Epictetus*[15]

Frederick Winslow Taylor was a mechanical engineer. He was born in Pennsylvania in 1856, and his early life was shaped by the culture and religion in which he was raised. Born into a Quaker family, Taylor experienced the egalitarian doctrine growing up, which states that people have power within themselves to commune with their God. The Quakers believe that there was no need for an intercessory, such as priest or saint to access God. Taylor believed this, too.

Taylor's mother was a descendent of the pilgrims, and we can safely assume she carried that pedigree with some pride. More importantly, the legacy of the pilgrims is one of religious quest that manifested in the seeking of a new land for a fresh start.

Young Fredrick Taylor was hit with a double dose of independence. Firstly, he was taught independence in the internal world of religion via the Quakers. He was also taught the can-do pioneering philosophy of the

Pilgrims. But Taylor also had a third hit, his community of Germantown, Pennsylvania, known for its work ethic, efficiency, and community structure.

Bright, educated, and focused, Taylor passed the Harvard examination and was admitted. Frederick Winslow Taylor was a combination of a generational structure and orderly behavior. Externally, his trajectory appeared as predictable as the changing seasons. However, Taylor zigged when all the signs of his upbringing told us he would zag.

Taylor followed the traditional pattern at the time, working shop floors and then transitioning through the age-old system of apprentice, journeyman, and craftsman. He learned his craft and did it well. He moved through the ranks swiftly using his intelligence and work ethic to advance. Through his education, his upbringing and keen sense of observation, Taylor went on to develop methods of managing work and workflow. He was the advocate of "The One Best Way."

Taylor's key work, *The Principles of Scientific Management*, was published in 1911 when he was age fifty-five, just four years before his death. The key points of Taylor's principles of scientific management are:

1. Replace rule-of-thumb, or ad hoc work methods, with methods based on a scientific study of the particular tasks.
2. Scientifically select, train, and develop each employee, instead of leaving them to train themselves as they saw fit.
3. Provide instruction as well as supervision of each worker as they do their job.
4. Divide work nearly equally between managers and workers.

The intent was for managers to employ scientific management principles planning work, and then have workers actually perform the job.

Taylor's publication changed the world of work, and in turn, the very structure of how we see the world and interact with it. His work was about streamlining acts, creating efficiencies, and ensuring that everybody, workers and managers, produced at a maximum level. Through his economy of motion theory, he believed there was a proper way to pick up a box, turn and set it down. The idea of The One Best Way excludes all other ways as inferior, because by definition there can only be One Best Way.

Delving into the mystical path involves work, study, observation and experience. At the entry level, it incorporates rules similar to what Taylor championed. Yet, at a certain point the experience becomes unique.

Seeking The One Best Way

Some mystics who also teach their way will tell you that you need to, for example, put your hands on your thighs while you practice. Others teachers will expand on what's already been taught and say, "That particular way is good. However, you need to put your hands further down your thighs for a deeper experience." And then the third mystic says, "Yes that is good, however your palms need to face the sky."

How do you know what the best way is for you? Should my hands be further down my thighs? Should my palms face upward?

There is an assumption that in reading this book you have had some religious and spiritual experiences. So one method of finding your discipline lies in this: Go back to your youth, to your earliest religious experiences. This is where you find your discipline. When you are a child, the only thing you have is faith. You have faith that your parents are going to feed you, and you have faith that your house will be warm. When you engage in a religious experience when all you have is faith, that religious experience becomes part of your core. This is where you go to find the beginning of your path. If you were raised Catholic, seek the Catholic path. If you were raised Anglican, seek the Anglican path. If you were raised Presbyterian, seek the Presbyterian path. These are the places where you have that very first, seminal experience of faith. All things move from this initial religious position, where you go from this base understanding is optional.

For example, it would be difficult to bring Hindu practice into a Christian practice, because they are different modalities. You could put a Chevrolet engine in a Rolls Royce automobile, but you would have to do a lot of work to make it fit. However, the car may never work quite right. This is because the Rolls Royce is designed differently than the Chevrolet: the construction methods are different, the materials are different, and ultimately the person who purchases a Rolls Royce instead of a Chevrolet is a different customer.

So your childlike introduction into religion, based on the faith experience, leads one down the path of a modality. In this instance, we are speaking specifically about the Christian experience. The core principles of the Christian religion are sacrosanct; the methods in addressing the experience can vary, yet they still address the basic core principles.

Look at your childhood faith with adult eyes and with an adult mind. View it with a new perspective, and hear the words that are spoken as an adult. Look at the art in an adult way. As an adult, join the adult with the child's faith.

The Choices You Make

Ask any parishioner if they are worshiping at the best church. Their answer will be, "Yes." Ask any parishioner if they are participating in the best version of Christianity, and their answer is again likely to be, "Yes". But the more thoughtful answer will be, "Yes, it is the best for me."

If you ask people that have been to Las Vegas and gambled the standard question, "How did you do?" the answer is most often, "I broke even," or, "Well, I broke even, if you take into the account the complimentary room." The fact is that Las Vegas was not built on people breaking even. This rationalization of choice takes place every day. We buy cars and always say, "I got a great deal."

Where do you buy gas for your car? There is little doubt that these purchases and others are made within a seven-minute radius from your home. It's likely that you consider the grocery store in your neighborhood a good grocery store and that it carries every item you want or desire. But does carry what you need? There is a big difference. You would not shop at that your local store if it didn't meet your basic needs. Your local church may not meet your basic needs, or it may. This is an answer that you must find out for yourself.

Expectations

> *"Treat a man as he is and he will remain as he is.*
> *Treat a man as he can and should be and he will become*
> *as he can and should be."*
>
> - *Stephen R. Covey*[16], *The 7 Habits of Highly Effective*
> *People: Powerful Lessons in Personal Change*

External Expectations

Assumptions and expectations can place demands on you as you walk this journey, especially if you decide to make a public pronouncement or reveal your experience. Christian mystics from the past chose to do both.

Julian of Norwich (1342-1423) lived as an anchoress in a Benedictine community. An anchoress is a woman who lives in a cell attached to a church or monastery. Julian of Norwich committed her life to contemplation and prayer, staying in that one place, her cell, until her death. The more modern and public Thomas Merton (1915 - 1968) wrote and published many books during his lifetime. He traveled the world and participated in conferences with other religious leaders. Both Julian and Merton left great works, yet did so in different ways. Neither of these people kowtowed, acted out of fear of retribution, but submitted willingly and in that submission found a form of freedom.

The media often propagates these assumptions, and people accept these assumptions because it is easy to do so. The assumptions are presented as the easily accessible archetypes and the icons designed to be accessed and understood upon initial contact. We are human and more complex than this, and we are also spiritual beings that have multifaceted experiences that are difficult to communicate. And as Julian and Merton demonstrate standardization of presentation is not a requirement.

Internal Expectations

Your internal expectations are likely to be more stringent than those placed on orders and those placed by society on you. Your internal expectations should answer questions with one of five answers.

1. What is the correct answer?
2. Yes
3. No
4. I will find out
5. No excuse

Internal dialogue can be dominated by circuitous dances of fancy and ego. To avoid this cerebral dance, the five answers are a great first cut to use in order to separate meaningless chatter from a productive path.

The Instinctual Human

"Some one dear to one can be loved with human love; but an enemy can only be loved with divine love."

- *Leo Tolstoy*[17]

Let's take a local government official that has caused you a problem and made your life a little harder. Seal them up into a steel cage. Then put a couple of windows in the cage to ensure your offender can see you, but they cannot reach you. Then berate them by swearing at them, call them names and give them the finger, if you want to. When you are done, you can walk away, the government official will never know your name and never catch up with you, and you have complete anonymity. Would you do it? The idea should be distasteful, yet we do it in our automobiles. The moment of anger is based on the instinctual act, and the knowledge that we can get away with it, and there is no recourse. If someone were to act in the same way while waiting in line at the bank, it would be a major disturbance with security and even the police getting involved.

The instinctual human is defined as a person who experiences the world through the five basic senses: sound, taste, touch, sight, and smell. These are the dependable forms of experience that the instinctual human has.

57

Something must come through one of these five senses for an experience to be valid. If an experience takes place outside of these five listed avenues, the knowledge is often rejected.

The instinctual human does not engage in structured meditation as a rule, but may do so as the choice is always available. Through this they may access contemplation, an aspect of the instinctual human that is almost always engaged. The contemplative focus of the instinctual human is not a philosophical or spiritual form. The focus of the instinctual man's contemplation is about resource. The acquisition and the management of resources are essential to human existence. Without the trait of resource management, the body will die or fail to reproduce, both of which are base drives that must be addressed.

To explore the immutable rule of resource procurement, let's look at the human desire to procure fats in our daily diet. The reason that the body wants fats is because they are rich in nutrition, and nutrients are needed for existence. Furthermore, the body will take as much as it can of this nutrient because availability is not, historically, consistent or dependable. In much of the world, people have little option to move beyond the state of instinctual existence, because safe food and drinking water are driving factors in the choices made in a day.

In 1976, while I was taking a class on Current World Problems, a student asked our teacher, a Vietnam veteran, "Why would the Vietnamese people embrace communism? It doesn't make any sense."

He replied, "When you are hungry, you don't care who is feeding you."

Having enough resources in life and having these basic needs met is a wonderful gift, allowing for a level of mental freedom, an opportunity to spend conscious effort in contemplative thought around subjects other than food, water, and procreation. However, it's not always the case that a person who has these basic needs met will turn their contemplation or thoughts in the direction of the Divine.

Because the instinctual human has a bounty come their way through their material contemplation, they can carry that behavior upward into the next level of existence. This projection of behavior makes sense, as he's been successful using the tools of contemplation for material gain. He's confident that those same tools will continue to work on a bigger scale or in different environment.

This is the instinctual human's thought extension. This extension brings greater resource to the five senses. There is a width and depth of the five senses that cannot be exceeded, yet the instinctual human will make every effort to find new ways of experiencing the world through volume and content.

The instinctual human may well live a fine life but will never grow into their true nature as designed by The Creator.

Maslow Triangle

Maslow's Hierarchy of Needs

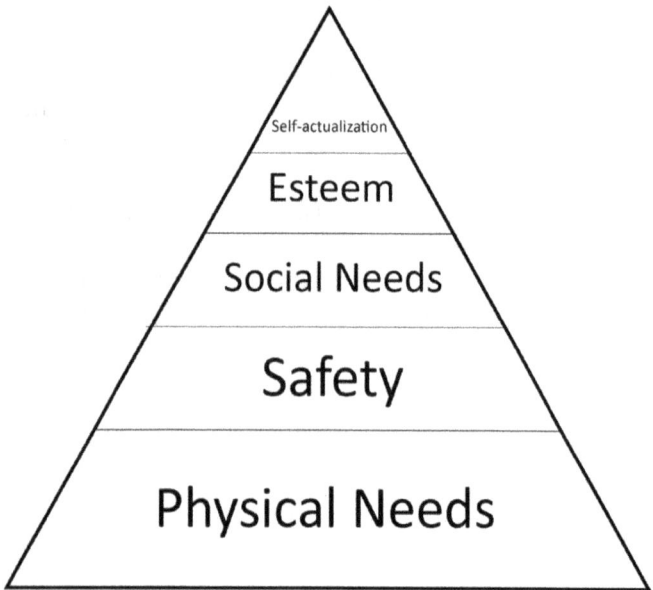

Self-actualization

Esteem

Social Needs

Safety

Physical Needs

The Enhanced Human

Self-Actualization is the intrinsic growth of what is already in the organism, or more accurately, of what the organism is."

- Abraham Maslow[18]

Abraham Maslow was an American psychologist, known for his Maslow's Hierarchy of Needs. His theory is illustrated below. As you move from the bottom of the triangle to the top, the illustration shows the way one's basic needs are met. Maslow believed that people are complex and are a combination of aspects of this hierarchy.

A key take away from Maslow is that people that fall into the normal range of human existence for their place and time have a coherence in their life.

Maslow was a proponent of what he called self-actualization. Here's how he explained this concept:

"What a man can be, he must be. This need we may call self-actualization...It refers to the desire for self-fulfillment, namely, to the tendency for him to become actualized in what he is potentially. This tendency might be phrased as the desire to become more and more what one is, to become everything that one is capable of becoming."

- Abraham Maslow

Some of the other aspects of Maslow's work are for a deeper study and are not covered in this book. His work is easily accessible for free, and readily available for your own research.

Characteristics of Self-Actualizing People

One aspect of actualizing people is that they are realistic about how they see the world. Acceptance is another aspect of self-actualizing people. These people accept themselves, acknowledge regrets, and are not inhibited while keeping social norms in mind. These people also are individuals and see themselves as such. They are interested in personal growth and take actions to move in the direction growth on a continual basis.

A third aspect is, that, without exception, self-actualized people are devoted to something larger than themselves. They have a mission, a calling, and an imperative in life that they must pursue.

The fourth aspect is their need for privacy. They are often alone, but not lonely. Self-actualized people have a self-referring aspect to their make-up. External acknowledgement is nice to these people but not necessary. These characteristics extend to a sense of, appreciation for, the big in life as well as the small.

The Mystical Road Map

"I shall be telling this with a sigh
Somewhere ages and ages hence:
Two roads diverged in a wood, and I—
I took the one less traveled by,
And that has made all the difference."

          - *Robert Frost*[19], *The Road Not Taken*

Scaramelli begins his work by breaking the human existence into two parts, two roads with separate destinations. These two parts consist of the human existence without meditation and the human existence with meditation.

One summer while working in the National Forest I found myself working on a reforestation crew. The work was hard and some of the people working on the crew had deep criminal backgrounds. Break time conversations often began with the phrase, "My parole officer says…" Working the thick duff of the forest floor we had to use a shovel before we could get to the planting soil with the hoe and then plant a pine tree seedling. The guy I was teamed with still young but he was hard – and he didn't know how to use a shovel. The rain was coming down hard and with no rain gear we both quickly became waterlogged. I watched him struggle with the shovel; in an hour we would

63

trade roles but he was exhausting himself. He clearly had never learned to work a shovel correctly. "Hey, trade me." I held out the hoe. He looked at me through the heavy rain as if there was some agenda that he couldn't find the angle on. "You serious?" I held the hoe forward and we traded shovel for hoe. Once he had the shovel in hand he paused for a moment looked at me and said, "Fool," and then stood there waiting for me to dig. After a second, of sorting what had just happened, I thrust the shovel into the ground and dug making no comment.

The "instinctive human" exists without meditation. This person lives a life solely through the known senses of taste, touch, smell, vision and hearing. These five senses provide the total experience and understanding for the non-meditating, instinctive human. We could say that spiritually, he is a car that has never left the driveway; he remains parked.

Through meditation, the human experience crosses over into two subdivisions: acquired contemplation and infused contemplation.

Acquired contemplation means that any results or changes in the practitioner's views on life, mental capacities, or emotional stability are the direct result of making effort through the acts of disciplines, contemplation, and meditation.

Acquired contamplation is similar to a racetrack. A racetrack is contained, and it has a limited destination and a goal without ever seeing new terrain. Although quite enjoyable to the practitioner, the same experience is had over and over again, because there is a limit to how far the results of one's own efforts can progress them along the spiritual path.

The rational human's other meditative or contemplative experience is infused contemplation. Infused contemplation is transformational because the Holy Spirit acts on the practitioner; his understanding of existence is then enhanced.

Infused contemplation can be broken into three grades, each grade having a distinct quality yet not superior to any other grade:

1. Visions—this is literally seeing something that is trans-dimensional/non-corporeal in nature.

Famous examples are the visions at Fátima Portugal. In 1916, three children working as sheep herders claimed to experience visitations from an angel on several occasions. One of the children reported seeing a lady in the sky who was brighter than the sun and filled with religious symbology. Many other visions are associated with Fátima, such as the classic 1917 "Miracle of the Sun" seen by a crowd in excess of 30,000 people.

2. Locutions—these are private and internal auditory experiences without visions or apparitions as part of the experience.

Mahatma Gandhi, the man who almost single handedly achieved Indian independence from Britain, Gandhi listened to an inner voice. He believed the voice to be the voice of God for guidance. "It may be a product of my heated imagination. If it is so, I prize that imagination as it has served me for a chequered life extending over a period of now nearly over fifty-five years..."

3. Revelation—this is defined as the unveiling of a hidden truth via an infusion.

Revelations can sometimes be infused with apocalyptic sensibilities, such as the Bible's last book, "Revelation." For our purposes, a revelation is to have something revealed in a dramatic fashion that has not been known before.

Of these three grades, there are sub-divisions that identify qualities that each possesses, with the exception of revelation (revelation ends and cannot be subdivided into further expressions of the experience).

The first grade of contemplation, visions, is broken down into three distinct groups. They are:

1. Corporeal vision
2. Imaginary vision
3. Intellectual vision

Corporeal Vision

"Youth is easily deceived because it is quick to hope."

- *Aristotle*[20]

It was near midnight, the high school party had gotten out of control about a half an hour ago, and now the late arrivals added a violent element. These latecomers were disturbed, aggressive and ready to fight. Before too long, one of them knocked a skinny teenager to the ground and was savagely beating him.

Foolishly, two of us rushed forward to stop the fight. Unable to pull the attacker off the teenager, my buddy turned, grabbed a decorative rock the size of a cantaloupe from an adjacent flower bed, and smashed the rock down into the back of the attacker. The rock bounced off. The attacker leaped to his feet, wheeled around, and hit me before I could respond. A flash of blue exploded in my field of vision. Moments later, I awoke to the sensation of wet grass on the side of my face. I had just experienced a corporeal vision.

A corporeal vision is considered the least of the three forms of visions and has no real significance. As the name implies, these type of visions are of the body and are not spiritual in nature. The reason they seem unique or special is that they lack a clear origin. However they

67

come from the body, but in a form that is not an average experience, hence the experiencer is predisposed to crediting something other than the body as the source of the moment.

Being knocked out, by say a boxer, has a clear origin and is not mistaken for a spiritual experience.

Corporeal visions are the more common of visions and require a good understanding of their origin. Corporeal visions are experiences of the senses that can sometimes appear to be divine because the content does not necessarily match the context. These visions appear to be unique. They are uncommon and not part of our normal existence. Yet they are indeed normal.

There are ways to discern whether you are experiencing a corporeal vision. They last for just a few moments. Since these visions are unique to a person's everyday experience, they can take on an importance that they really don't deserve. These visions are similar to seeing an exotic animal, say a peacock, for the first time. Because these birds are unique, they can be given more attention than is deserved. They stimulate the curiosity of the viewer, the stimulation is seen as compelling, and the emotions legitimatize the moment.

The brain is the keeper of the five senses. It sits encased in total darkness using only the body's senses to interpret the world. The fingers, ears, nose, tongue, and eyes are the tools that the brain uses to sense the world. The combination of these senses with the brain as interpreter of the world results in a magnificent recipe for a world constructed in ways that you wish to see it. The only partially exposed part of the brain are the eyes, and they are part of an imperfect system of capturing what is happening around you. The brain and these eyes are consistently conspiring to tell you little lies to make your life easier.

The neurological bundle at the back of the eye feeds down the optic nerve to the brain to create the blind spot in the human vision field. This blind spot is physiological—the bundle of nerves is void of cones and rods, the two elements design to pick up color, light and shadow for the human eye. The human brain actually takes artistic license and fills in this blind spot. The brain makes assumptions based on the surrounding elements, adjacent information, and past experience to hide what would otherwise be a disturbing hole in your field of vision.

You can discover your own blind spot by taking a piece of paper and drawing two dots on the paper about six inches apart. Now hold the paper against your nose, close one eye and look at the paper to the dot in front of the closed eye. Now push the paper away slowly from your face, soon one of the dots will disappear. This dot is now in your eye's blind spot. But your brain moves right past the fact that it can't see the dot and creates blank paper where there is actually a dot. This is your brain lying to you to force the world to make sense.

Your brain not only makes up information that may be missing, the brain also throws information away. Take your right hand and hold it out in front of your face, extending your hand out to arms length, and hold your index finger up. If you look directly at your index finger, it is quite easy to see. Now, keep your eyes straight ahead and begin to move your right arm to the right. Slowly you will get to a place in your vision where you can tell that there is a hand at the end of your arm but you cannot determine how many fingers are being held up. Your peripheral vision is very good at sensing motion it is horrific at allowing analysis.

Your brain makes up what it thinks is important. The blind spot causes you to invent missing information, and your peripheral vision throws away too much information to sort out what is really going on. Your brain is constantly creating lies of inclusion and exclusion. The brain is interested in making decisions that will aid you in surviving the day, and this method of inclusion and exclusion is a tried and true method.

Seeing something in your peripheral vision brings a very simple response: using fight-or-flight for survival. The natural choice is to make more distance and protect with a flinch. This flinch reaction to danger is a deep emotional response. For instance, peripheral vision doesn't see a snake and proceed to analyze, "Is that a coral snake, or is that a bull snake?" No! The peripheral vision says, "Snake!" and tells the brain to create distance quickly. This fight-or-flight trigger has a built in generator called the "adrenal dump," a chemical cocktail dilates the pupils of the eyes, increases muscle strength, and limits communication between the left and right hemispheres of the cerebral cortex. You are left with deep, meaningful, root emotions, and reactions that instantly sear deep into the brain.

You see with your peripheral vision throughout your waking hours, and you dismiss most of what happens. However, when the motion is out of the ordinary, the peripheral vision goes into action. You are lied to via exclusion, lied to by the inclusion. Now, with information that is suspect, add the adrenal dump, the fight-or-flight reaction, and you can see that a corporal vision is born of an unreliable mother.

Here's another example. Try to read the word five places to the right without moving your eyes to experience the true area of focus you have with your vision. When you're reading, your focus is only the size of a dime, the brain is continually throwing information away it is continually saying, "That's not needed, and we've experienced that other stuff. Time to move on." Here's another example: There are hundreds of thousands of versions of chairs, yet you only really need to sit on a chair once or twice before you understand the basic shape. Your brain understands the master structure of a chair. It can decide whether it is safe for you to sit on it or not.

Examples of obfuscated vision—nearsightedness (myopia), farsightedness (hyperopia), clouding of the cornea (cataracts), and floaters (myodesopsia) demonstrate that your visual sense does a fantastic job of moving you through the world on a daily basis. The human visual system may misfire on occasion, but we can still make sense of our world.

The human brain is designed to see itself, to seek commonality in the world. This drive for facial recognition is so hard wired that two symbols used in the English written word, the colon, and the bracket. When we unite the colon and the bracket we create the smiley face punctuation used in text communication a million times a day. To further emphasize the recognition factor, note that the two symbols are oriented 45 degrees from how they are found in nature, yet we still recognize the face smiling at us from the screen. :) This little example demonstrates that the brain make leaps in information for you. Further, the brain will also try and make something anthropomorphic, give an object human characteristics.

Any human being, regardless of discipline or effort, may have a corporeal vision. It is the way that they deal with the experience that is important. The instinctive human will not ponder the event or make too much of it, as it has little to do with the here and now. The immediate experience of satisfying needs for existence is paramount. People that are engaged in contemplation are likely to give some level of weight to these types of experiences.

It is important to make an attempt to understand the

origins of such experiences, acknowledging them for what they are. Corporeal visions warrant a quick audit and then are usually dismissed as one dismisses a crazy dream once they realize that the cause was eating spicy food before retiring to bed. Corporeal visions should be treated, in the same way. They carry as much meaning as a silly dream and should be given the same amount of your time and thought.

Imaginary Vision

On the third day of a Zen meditation retreat, we were practicing sitting in seiza in the old theater on the decommissioned military base. Seiza is a classic way of Japanese sitting, meaning, literally, "proper way sitting". Imagine your legs folded underneath and kneeling to have a visual of seiza.

The mornings were cold when we awoke at the retreat, the meals austere, and there was no speaking permitted, except during designated times. As I sat on the little wooden seiza bench, after a time a new world opened up to me. I felt the top of my head split open as if it were a crisp apple cleaved by a kitchen knife. It took me to a new place, a world composed of high mountains and deep valleys. The mountains and valleys seemed familiar, yet they also had significantly different properties. Sailing quickly through the valleys, it was as if I was a ray of light. I had no wings, no body, and I was only my mind moving as fast as my thoughts.

Vibrant colors began to fly at me. They had an energy behind them that is indescribable. Each color was alive. I was in awe. I sat there dumbstruck and elated at the same time. Then, as clear as someone sitting across the table from me, I heard a voice in my head tell me, "These are the things that are truly important."

At that instant, I was shot forward, faster than I had been before. The colors began to blend, the mountains and the valleys flew by, and I was no longer able to keep my focus. If I could comprehend the speed of light, this was it. My mind was now moving faster. It was completely aware of what was going on, and yet I was completely unable to control any aspect of it.

Then, just as unexpectedly as it began, the moment ended abruptly, as if somebody had walked over and pulled a lamp plug out of the wall. Everything went dark. Opening my eyes, I was thrilled by what happened. I sat still, trying to comprehend and contemplate the events. It was vital that I find the meaning of what had happened.

After some time, the deep roar of the gong signaled the end of the meditation session. This was a time where I was permitted to speak, so I sought out one of the instructors and explained my profound experience.

The instructor listened intently, with his eyes still focused on the group, and nodded occasionally to what I was saying. When I finished, he was silent. I stood waiting for his response. He finally turned to me and said, "Go back and sit. This will pass." I was amazed, and my ego was infuriated. "This was a profound experience, one of great value, I need help interpreting this!" my ego screamed in my head.

I got some water and waited for the gong to signal the beginning of the next session. "OK," I thought, "this is what I am supposed to do, and I'll do it. But I think that my vision was real and important, and I'm going to go find it." I closed my eyes and breathed, militantly like a child breathes after being told to eat their vegetables.

Years later, that vision never returned. The vision I had seemed real; however, it turned out that the direction given by the teacher was important and the vision was not. The word "imaginary" is used to mean "unreal, unbelievable, or something that occurs inside the mind of the individual." And this is just what I experienced, an imaginary vision.

The teacher that day was well aware of the experiences that people have at about seventy-two hours into such a retreat, and he also knew that the moments people have at this time are unlikely to be valid. Imaginary visions are a fanciful creation of the brain that has been deprived of stimulation turning in on its self to find something to focus on, to compare, and contrast.

Brian Keenan is the author of *An Evil Cradling*, a book about his four years as a hostage in Beirut. He talked to the BBC for their show *Horizon*, about isolation, and he touched on the sensations he experienced when he was deprived of sensory input from being held in the dark for many months. "I can remember one distinctly, 'cus it was dreadfully lucid and clear. It was about being alone in a desert and being very, very hot, and then being instantly bone-numbingly cold. Having the winds of the desert stripping away, as if you could feel your flesh falling off ya. And so you were left as a bony hulk in the corner."

The brain, when deprived of sensory input, will create stimulation. This stimulation is real, but the results are not. No action should be not taken as a result of an imaginary vision. It is far easier to say this in the context of the controlled environment such as a meditation retreat. It is, of course, much more difficult to say such things in the context of the sort of kidnapping that Keenan experienced. As a testament to the power of this experience, Keenan went on to say that he feared the visions more than the guns his captors brandished.

Intellectual Vision

"Knowing belongs to man's intellect or reason; loving belongs to his will.
The object of the intellect is truth; the object of the will is goodness or love."

- *Fulton J. Sheen*[22]

Rene Descartes, the famous French philosopher, mathematician and writer, developed the habit of lying in bed until very late in the morning to use the time for contemplation. As Descartes he lay there, he watched a fly buzzing over his head, dancing between the walls and the ceiling. At that moment, as simple as can be, coordinate geometry just came to him. In a fully appreciated intellectual vision, Descartes realized that he could find the location of the fly by measuring the x and y axes, in this case, the wall and the ceiling.

Intellectual vision is clear and certain. This type of vision makes sense to the mind. There is little effort needed to figure out what was meant in the experience. The attributes of intellectual vision can be direct as a clear picture, or manifest symbolically. Regardless of how it appears to the mind, there is no hesitation as to the subject or meaning of the experience. In other words, if you need to analyze a situation and ask, "What does this mean?" it is not an intellectual vision. Intellectual visions are explicit, clear, and leave no doubt.

The intellectual vision is the default, a catch-all descriptor used by people as they try to communicate the ineffable moment that interrupts their normal existence and brings them some form of unique message. Even when people have different modes of receiving the communication, say, they heard a voice tell them something, they will still often use the word "vision" to describe the moment.

The intellectual vision is devoid of symbolisms and sound. It is a knowing that does not have an anchor in the five senses. An example of this is might be that a Catholic, holding an icon of the Virgin Mary in reverence, may experience the fragrance of roses that are often associated with the Divine Mother. This, of course, is an example of activating only one of the five senses. This type of sensory ignition, or interaction, is unlikely to be part of a intellectual vision.

People will describe the intellectual vision as a simple knowing. This experience is often given a slang term of "women's intuition" or a "gut feeling." Often, the phrase, "It's hard to explain," is used in front of the attempt to describe intellectual vision. "I don't know why" is also a common way of explaining and not explaining at the same time, the phrases, or versions of the phrases, "I don't know," and, "I can't explain it," are verbal indicators of intellectual vision. Simply put intellectual visions are beyond words.

Experiencing intellectual visions in a beneficial way is often an acquired skill. In childhood, when intellectual visions often manifest and are not discouraged, the skill of judgment and discrimination will grow and become a useful tool throughout life. Often the encouragement is casual. For instance, a simple question from a father to a son might be something like, "What does you gut tell you?" Or a mother might instruct her daughter to "listen to what your intuition tells you." Or perhaps one could caution their friend, "Trust that your first reaction was correct."

Attunement, which is the ability to discern the indicators of a valid intellectual vision, is a skill that must be nurtured and grown. As one becomes more practiced and skilled, such discernment of validity against the fevered ramblings of the body's neurological system can be achieved.

Sacred and Profane

The difference between intuition and intellectual vision is that intuition is set in the profane, and intellectual vision is set in the sacred. Profane is used in this sense in the traditional use, as separate from sacred. Profane is not automatically vulgar.

Yet the intuition and intellectual vision are not mutually exclusive. As with almost all extra-sensory moments, the line between the categories can be blurred. The context in which these things happen is important for helping to determine the sanctity of the moment.

Sigmund Freud, the famous founder of psychoanalysis, used the interpretation of symbols, especially in dreams, as keys to the psyche of a person. Freud was also known for smoking cigars. As the story goes after a lecture about phallic symbolism, an audience member asked Freud about his own cigar and its relation to the human phallus. Freud was reported as replying that, "Sometimes a cigar is just a cigar." Research points to the fact that the story is not likely true, but the story has truth. Sometimes things are what they are and nothing more. But this is all determined by the context in which these moments occur.

An intellectual vision at the conclusion of a religious service—where the music, prayers, lighting of candles and incense literally change the brain's attunement. An intellectual vision at this moment can bear meaning.

The sacred, and the activities associated with the sacred, change the functionality of the brain.

Philosophers and psychologists have discussed the construct of the human mind and the human brain over many centuries. Their predominant position is that the mind stands outside of the brain. Consciousness and the perception of one's experiences are a function of the mind. This is not a new concept—It's an ancient concept that comes to the western world via Plato (427 - 347 BC). Plato felt that the mind was its own entity and was the seat of consciousness, with the brain serving as an interface by which the mind exerts its will.

Aristotle (384 -322 BC) had a different view. His position was that the mind served as a label used to bring together a group of mental actions that don't have a high level of commonality into a nice, tidy package of mental function.

Most mystics of the world favor Plato's viewpoint. The famous Christian mystic St. Francis of Assisi considered the body, "Brother Ass." The word Brother, of course, designates a separation between mind and body. The ass was the automobile of the day and the means of travel. So it's obvious that Francis considered his body separate from who he was.

Locutions

One day, my babysitter was not my babysitter anymore.
As a small child, I didn't know what was going on. It was
never discussed. She just didn't come anymore. It wasn't
until later years that I found out how she became my ex-
babysitter. She stabbed her husband in the shoulder blade
while he ate breakfast. He was not critically hurt, but it
was still a shocking event. When asked why she stabbed
her husband, she said, "God told me to." She had a
locution, likely an imaginary locution.

The word locution is narrow in its uses and is rarely
used in general conversation. It is a word used in the
discussion of hearing the Divine Voice by some religious
groups. So you can see by its nature it is not a popular
word, but well suited here.

The word is of Latin origin meaning an utterance or
a spoken word. So a locution is simply a word or phrase
spoken to another. For our purposes we have two forms of
locutions, the imagery and the intellectual. When used in
the context of a mystical experience, it enters into a new

realm, because the implication is that you, the listener, are hearing an utterance from somewhere other than from another corporeal human being. The earmarks of a locution are that it is generally singular in nature, only one person hears the locution. There are cases of a group of people hearing a voice such as in the Garabandal apparitions in 1961 through 1965 where several young people heard the Archangel Michael and The Virgin Mary. A locution is auditory, but it generates no sound waves; it is heard in the listener's mind and not with the ears, yet sounds as if the ears have heard the words. Locutions can occur spontaneously during common activities in the day, but are frequently heard within the context of prayer. As prayer sets the mind, the intent is present, and the time can be right for a locution to be heard.

There is no presence or any other entity present in the same space during a locution. Nothing serves as the vehicle for the communication. A vision, by its name and nature, has an image attached serving as a focal point for the message. There is no apparent focal point for a locution.

My babysitter had a locution that asked her to stab her husband. Any locution that tells you to harm another is a lie. The lie can be biological, generated by your nervous system, or demonic.

History is rife with examples of visions and locutions telling people to do harm to others. In 1966, Charles Whitman killed his wife and his mother. Whitman then climbed to the top of the University of Texas clock tower. Before he was killed by officer Houston McCoy, Whitman shot an additional 15 people to death from the tower, and wounded 32.

Whitman penned a note that requested an autopsy of his body. The coroner found a congenital necrotic tumor. Whitman was born with this tumor, and it had been shrinking. However, the growth of the blood flow to the tumor swelled the area, pressing against the amygdala. As mentioned earlier, this area of the brain is responsible for the fight-or-flight response. It is likely that Whitman's horrible acts had a physiological cause.

In 2001 Jennifer Cisowski killed her 8-month-old son, fearing demonic possession and citing numerous biblical references as her reasoning for this heinous act. According to reports, Cisowski heard a voice that told her to test her faith by harming her baby. The voice guaranteed the child would return from the dead. Cisowski told investigators that she knew it was wrong to harm the baby, but she threw the baby onto the stones by the pool, nevertheless. Jennifer told investigators that a "spirit" voice told her to harm the baby as a test of faith. She was quoted as saying, "Just like Jesus raised Lazarus, I threw the baby on the stones..."

Biological or demonic, any voice that tells you to harm another in any context is not of God. It must be rejected summarily and immediately. Further, seek help immediately at all available levels and forms: professional, medical, and religious.

Imaginary Locutions

Imaginary locutions can be heard at any time. They are not restricted to meditation, contemplation, or prayer.

If an imaginary locution can be summoned at your will, it is not real. There is a difference between recalling a moment via memory and summoning up a new imaginary locution. An imaginary locution however can be helpful in the right context, say the helpful words of a coach gone over by an athlete prior to a game, and the words heard in the coaches voice. This type of summing is done on a daily basis when you read the words of a close friend and hear the words in their voice.

Intellectual Locutions

Pure understanding is the shortest way to describe intellectual locutions. The attributes that sets this experience apart are the lack of visual characteristics and voice. The intellectual locution is heard. There is a sense of understanding that is clearly a gift from the domain of the Divine. A certain phrasing or a special characteristic reaches the person. This special characteristic could be nestled in the message, a regional colloquialism, a vernacular from childhood, or a term that is specific to the person's work.

Carlos Santana has sold millions of music albums, gaining gold and platinum albums over his long career. After his marriage of many years failed, he tried to commit suicide, not once but several times. In a 2008 Rolling Stone magazine interview Santana talked about the locution that saved him at his moment of crisis.

> *"But each time I would go light up a candle, and I'm still hearing all this inner stuff, a thousand voices screaming at you, accusing you... but then I would just look at a picture of Jesus and say, 'Help me,' and then, very clearly, inwardly, I would hear this one voice that's softer and louder than all the others, and it would say, 'I'm sitting next to you. Isn't that enough?'*

> *"Once I heard that voice, something would shift, and I'd be able to find joy again in food and breathing."*

The Divine Voice

The Divine Voice is the realm of God and of God's agents, angels, and saints.

In this case, the voice that is heard demands immediate action, not necessarily by an explicit command but by the power of the experience. The hearing of the Divine Voice is contextually important, so as a rule, messages received by beginners in contemplative practice should be given low regard by the recipient and also the mentor. If the beginner on this journey experiences the Divine Voice, it is likely that it is not the Divine Voice. Because the experience should be treated with some level of respect, as it is extraordinarily powerful to the beginner, yet the voice has little importance. The idea that a person can experience beginner's luck is almost always invalid.

Separating the person from the experience is essential. In other words, the experience does not make them particularly special, yet it validates the person. Approaching the experience with skepticism is very important. At this point, an outright rejection may be appropriate but not always the first tool of counsel whether by self, of preferably by a spiritual director. To adopt the idea that an initial experience is valid is convenient thinking in that it allows us to be enamored with the experience. It is an easy method that allows us to walk past the hard questions that such an experience requires.

There are guidelines that aid in the determining whether a Divine Voice is actually generated by the Divine or produced from one's own mind in an internal conversation.

Produced: There will be some attachment to a fantasy that is contemplated and focused upon. It will appear that the Divine Voice is making comment on the fantasy that is held in the mind, and that the Divine Voice is validating and directing the fantasy from within.

Hyper Focus: If a voice is heard, it can be the result of hyper focus on a particular subject or object, and this focus can result in a false voice. This is not to say that focus always manifests in a false voice. A produced voice, however, is not an uncommon product from this state of this concentration.

Explicit: The message will be explicit, direct, and have clear directives. It is often part of the realm of deception, "If you do this, then that will happen." The tell-tail aspect of this deception is the expression of the linear cause and effect. This message strokes the ego, which can be the dance hall of the demonic. True Divine Voice has subtlety. The words may contain a poetic quality as the message moves below the words. The message often has a deeper meaning and is expressed in a non-linear, overarching strategic way other than explicit commands.

Internal Conversation: If a Divine Voice is produced by an internal conversation, mental chatter will interrupt the voice. This is a sign that the utterance is false and generated, not infused.

Summing: If the Divine Voice is brought forth at will by your will, then it is false. The true Divine Voice can only be received, or requested and heard by the will of God.

Surprise: The Divine Voice is heard quite unexpectedly. However, this surprise takes place in the realm of preparation through prayer and contemplation, the reaching upward toward God. This sets the formation so that the Divine can manifest when the terms are favorable. This doesn't exclude the concept of God breaking through at any moment.

Revelation

"People need revelation, and then they need resolution."

- Damian Lewis[25]

Handsome Lake was a Seneca Native American. Living in what is now New York State in the mid-1700's, he lived a typical life for his time. He became a warrior and joined the raiding parties against adjacent nations such at the Choctaw and Cherokee. Abnormal external factors placed his nation under stress during the American Revolution. At that time, British and American forces made attempts to get the Seneca involved in the war and take up arms against their enemy. Handsome Lake's nation was pulled to and fro in the political dance of resource and conquest. He became an alcoholic. Over time, his body was compromised and he began to waste away. He was a shell of a human being by the accounts of the time and was tended to by his relatives. In 1799, Handsome Lake got up from his bed, staggered to the door of his cabin, yelled from the threshold, "So be it," in his native tongue, and then collapsed. Handsome Lake was scooped up by his family and returned him to bed, believing that he would soon die. By his bedside, they waited for his inevitable death. As additional family members arrived, it became clear that Handsome Lake had no breath and no heartbeat. Yet when Blacksnake a relative and fellow Seneca tribal member began to examine Handsome Lake's body, he found a warm spot in the middle of the man's chest. The family stood back and waited for something, maybe death or possibly a spontaneous resuscitation. It was unknown territory, and no one had seen this before.

After a couple of hours, Handsome Lake regained consciousness. He returned to this world with a message, a revelation. Handsome Lake went to the tribal council and told them of a meeting with three men who were sent as messengers from the Creator. These three emissaries listed the evil practices that were taking the lives of his people.

Handsome Lake went on to have episodic visions. In one he was shown a moral code that listed such forms of misconduct, such as witchcraft, drunkenness, sexual promiscuity, and other things such as card playing. During this journey, Jesus appeared to him and told him, "Tell your people that they will become lost when they follow the ways of the white man." Blacksnake helped Handsome Lake record "The Code of Handsome Lake," which was published in 1850. This code is still practiced among the Seneca today.

In the Christian lexicon, it is impossible to escape the associations around the word "revelation." The last book of the sixty-six that comprise the Bible, "Revelation" is a powerful, mystical book that contains tales of doom, destruction, warfare, death, famine, and sickness. It is a powerful and visually charged manuscript.

Revelation as a concept is a disclosure of an absolute and complete vision that is unconditional. The symbolism can be subject to interpretation. Caution needs to be exercised when one feels that they have experienced a revelation. There may be many outcomes to a prophetic revelation. Within the Book of Revelation are The Four Horsemen of the Apocalypse. The first horse and horseman are described in the King James Version of the Bible: "… And I looked and behold, a white horse. He who sat on it had a bow, and a crown was given to him, and he went out conquering and to conquer." Some say that the first rider is The Conqueror and others claim he is Pestilence. And some say he is Righteousness and still others say he is Evil. The very nuance of the horse's gait can be symbolically important. If he is in a gallop, it can mean that the horse is set free to charge the line of the war. If the horse is in a canter, it can imply a firm control by the rider.

Interpretation is everything.

For our purposes, we want to set aside every attachment to, and precept you have about, the word revelation in respect to the book in the Bible. The Biblical version of the word has many apocalyptic images attached. We will use the word as it refers to the infusing you with, or the pouring into you from, God.

Revelations stand alone outside of the other experiences aforementioned. Since revelations are most often a combination of vision and locution with profound metaphor and mythos, it is very difficult to communicate the totality of the experience. Symbolically, you are drinking from a fountain that must be restrained, and you are only able to consume the water in small gulps. Much can be lost, and in our instance, more can be lost in attempting to relate the experience.

Revelations are rarely spontaneous and are frequently sought after. It is rare that people are struck down on the street, in the same way that Saul was on the road to Damascus. Use the word revelation judiciously, as it is emotionally charged and carries with it some two thousand years of presence in the Christian mind. Revelation is a word that is often used in spiritual conversation improperly, as revelations have some very specific attributes that are not part of other forms of mystical experience. Revelation is sometimes used when the word vision might be more appropriate.

A revelation has five basic constituents that are earmarks of the experience. The key aspects of Revelation are:

1. External Stressors

These include the loss of resources, in particular non-essentials such as recreational items, prideful objects, items that are attached to heart and hearth are taken away.

2. Internal Stressors

This refers to physical pain. Some common expressions of internal stressors include headaches, gout, joint pain, and gastric problems.

3. Appearance of Insanity

Because reactions to the world come from a different perspective, the label of absurdity, insanity, or just caulked up to odd behavior by an external observer may be placed on these people who have had such transformational moments.

4. Shift of World Vision

The person's perception of the world, how it was seen and what was once valued, changes permanently.

5. Spreadable.

The revelation must be accessible, resonate with others, and be easily communicated. Intellectual understanding is not a requirement.

External Stress

Just as Handsome Lake experienced the external stress of the push and pull of the British and Colonial imperialism in his native New York, Jack Wilson (Wovoka among his people) was having a similar experience in Nevada. Wilson, a Paiute native, witnessed the loss of the native ways and the pacification of his people. He had a vision of himself, in heaven, talking to God. Due to his spiritual training from a holy man, Wilson was able to translate his experience, and share what was a revelation with his people. In this revelation, processing external and internal stressors, appearance of insanity, permanent shift of world view, and spreadable, God told him that his people must love each other and should not fight. They must find a way to live in peace with the white man. Also, there must be an end to the old ways of war and grieving the death of others through self-mutilation. The result of Wilson's revelation was the adaptation of his message across western America and the beginning of the Ghost Dance. The Ghost Dance is a dance designed to reunite the living with the spirits of the ancestors and bring insight and peace.

In the Mediterranean at around 70 AD, the structure of the Roman Empire was expansive and brutal. Nero committed suicide, the Jews revolted against Rome, and Jerusalem was destroyed. The persecution of the Christians by the Romans began in 64 AD, and the Coliseum, which served as the entertainment capital of the world for violence and wanton death, was built. Roman rule expanded into the Balkans, Mesopotamia, and beyond. During this time of great distress, John of Patmos, a persecuted Christian, lived under the burden of exile. He had a revelation and wrote it down, and it became the final book of The Bible, The Book of Revelation.

External stress pushes the visionary towards the moment and acts as a fertile field for the message. The cynic would call it an exploitation of people during difficult times, and at the other end of the spectrum, the believer would call the revelation "A vision of deliverance." Handsome Lake and the emerging new nation, Jack Wilson and the pacification of his people, and John of Patmos, persecuted and exiled, all experienced external stress. External stress is a necessary component, a catalytic element of, revelation.

Internal Stress

Internal stress can take on many forms because humans can find creative ways to tear down their bodies, to create distress. Through this means, they often find a form of clarity. This is a fine line that once stepped over can be terminal. Ascetic behavior is deliberate. Whether self-flagellation, the beating of one's self with a whip or the act of fasting, it is all designed to create an internal environment that is conducive to a mystical experience.

Often the agents of change on the internal landscape appear to be spontaneous. They are not easily recognizable in their time but are revealed in hindsight. An example is the meltdown of a marriage. It's an all too common event, yet devastating to all involved. The external appearances might be seen as uneventful during the course of a divorce, but the internal landscape is like a post-nuclear landscape. Internal stressors can also be created by how they think others see them—inadequate, inept, or unfulfilled. These emotions can create and add to the internal stress of one's existence. They can also manifest in other ways, just as Handsome Lake's alcoholism reduced him to a shard of a human being.

Appearance of Insanity

If you ran through the span of emotions that the average three-year-old runs through in two minutes, you would be placed on medication or possibly institutionalized. Revelation is so life-changing that the person who experiences the revelation no longer behaves in familiar ways. They are not the person once known. And the fact of the matter is that they are frequently not the same brain type that has been familiar to the external world anymore. An example, but not the only one, could be changing from a hard-charging personality to a more "live and let live" attitude.

This change is often dismissed as insanity, or just plain crazy. Determining insanity is not the place of this book, and it is best left to the psychiatric professionals, as each state, or country has its own definition of legal insanity. However, in a court of law, the core elements for the insanity defense are almost equally universal. In order to prove that a person is legally insane, the defense must establish that a mental disease or defect made the person incapable of appreciating the nature and consequences of their actions. This is a far cry from simply acting odd in front of your neighbors.

Shift of World Vision

The world does not look the same to people that experience a revelation. They don't see the same things that other see in the same light. The focus of their world has shifted—many things that once meant something no longer do, and things that held little value may now become most important. It is virtually impossible to itemize the style and content of this shift, but it is profound, and it is permanent.

Spreadable

Revelation is spreadable. The content and style of the revelation resonates with other people at some level. The message of the revelation is transferable and understandable. Otherwise, a revelation is not spreadable and dies with the messenger. The Book of Revelation, (The Apocalypse of St. John) became transferable and spreadable when it was chosen to be included in The Bible. The Book of Revelation had the gravity and bandwidth to be sustained for hundreds of years, to be pushed forward generationally and with authority.

As for interpretation of The Book of Revelation, one view is a spiritual one that holds that the events in the Book are not specific historical events; rather, they are symbolic, representing the struggle of good against evil, God against Satan. Another view is the past view where the books prophecy has been fulfilled. Still another view is that it is a historical document, presented in symbols. Yet another is the futurist view, which sees the events as yet to come. This is only a cursory overview of four classic dissections of The Book of Revelation. Understanding can be problematic. In this instance, spreadbility is the less difficult of these two aspects. Interpretation quickly diverges as people place their world view onto the revelation in an attempt to make the information understandable and meaningful.

Shortcuts

There are no fast paths to the mystical experience. The journey can take years or it can appear to happen quickly, but it is actually following a pedestrian time of preparation. Remembering that time is meaningless to God can help us to keep a perspective on what is happening in our religious or spiritual experience. All things happen at an appropriate time, in an appropriate intensity, and at the appropriate volume.

For centuries, alchemists sought the Philosopher's Stone. The Philosopher's Stone was a legendary substance that had the ability to turn base metals into valuable metals such as gold. This stone took on other properties over time, even the property of granting immortality. The Philosopher's Stone was taken so seriously that even Sir Isaac Newton, the man who defined the Age of Reason, engaged in alchemy for years in an effort to seek the benefits of the Philosopher's Stone.

There is no Philosopher's Stone when it comes to the mystical experience. The experience of connecting with the Divine is based upon disciplined, incremental steps, as a commitment to the direction you have chosen.

Van Gogh's Sunflowers

Some people will look at Vincent van Gogh's famous painting, Sunflowers, and in an offhanded way, will comment, "I could paint that." Of course, the answer is, "No you can't." It may appear to be easy to do, but van Gogh's Sunflowers are explosions of creativity that came from hours and hours of work, failure, drudgery, anxiety, and, in his instance, pain.

These hours are necessary to prepare for the moment when these gorgeous paintings of sunflowers present themselves to the artist. Your journey on the mystical path could mimic Sir Isaac Newton's search for the Philosopher's Stone, with moments like Vincent van Gogh's creation of "Sunflowers." Seek like Newton, be attentive and dedicated, and prepare for van Gogh's Sunflowers.

Drugs

"Dope never helped anybody sing better or play music better or do anything better.

All dope can do for you is kill you - and kill you the long, slow, hard way. "

- Billie Holiday[27]

Drugs are used by many cultures to bring on altered states of consciousness and religious experiences. In North America, some Native American cultures use peyote. In South America they use Ayahuasca. These drugs are part of their culture, not yours. Using them without the proper preparation and guidance, and without the cultural support, which began at birth, renders your use of these drugs meaningless.

Opening the doors via these drugs or other culture-specific drugs is a formula for a pile-up on the expressway. Understand that this is not an anti-drug message—this is an anti-drug experience message. These drugs work, and they work well. But to leap into the experience without the cultural backing and support of skilled individuals, shamans, medicine men, or medicine women is the equivalent of opening the doors and windows of your home and welcoming any and all visitors. Some of these visitors will surely be tricksters, or worse, they could be demonic in nature. Without proper protection and guidance, you are easy prey.

Understand these drugs are appropriate for their culture, and it is an act of hubris to assume you can interject yourself into that experience.

Drink

"Alcohol may be man's worst enemy, but the Bible says love your enemy."

- Frank Sinatra[28]

Anything to excess is bad, and this includes drink. Some wine, some beer, even a distilled spirit can be consumed without detriment. However, moderation is the key. Some mystics simply abstain. They don't pass moral judgment as to the use of alcohol, and they don't argue for temperance. They simply abstain. This is based on the argument that alcohol is an impediment to the mystical experience, reducing the drinker's clarity and ability to discern events.

Too much alcohol can cloud the ability to make decisions. Image the classic illustration of a person facing a decision with a devil on one shoulder and an angel on the other. Too much alcohol can weaken one's resolve and result in focusing on the devil, not the angel. Although these symbols are a cartoonish, simplistic illustration, they carry an air of validity.

Mantra, Mudra, Mandala, or, Hands of Prayer and Stained Glass Windows

"We are symbols, and inhabit symbols."

- Ralph Waldo Emerson[29]

In the east, there are mantra, mudra, and mandala. These three things, in order, are sacred utterances, ritual gestures, and sacred symbols. The West has the respective symbols of prayer, hands of prayer, and icons.

Hands of Prayer

Hands of Prayer

The following are four forms and multiple tools used to experience the world of the Divine. The Eastern words are unusual to the Western reader. They may appear to be exotic yet familiar. The tools used fall into four categories:

Rhythmic - dancing
Auditory - drums
Austerity - deprivation of the body, such as fasting
Drugs - traditional and culturally appropriate drugs.

Prayer / Mantra

The mantra is a repeated set of words that is used to set the intent of the person using the prayer. The mantra may have an intellectual meaning in the actual words used. It also carries a vibration or tone that is used to set the body in motion, alter the state of the brain, and attune the focus of the mind. There are several forms of prayer such as:

Worship – the glorification of The Creator
Mercy – asking for forgiveness
Love – an expression of affection for and of God
Petition – asking for a need to be met
Gratitude - an acknowledgment and appreciation for anything that has been gifted

A prayer can be very similar to a mantra by tone, style, and method. An example of this is The Jesus Prayer, which is used across Christianity and favored by The Desert Fathers, the originators of Christian monasticism. The Jesus Prayer is a simple and yet profound prayer or mantra with several versions that vary in length and choice of word, but they never vary in intent. The prayer reads, "Lord Jesus Christ, Son of God, have mercy on me, a sinner."

The breakdown of this payer is dense and profound to the intellect. The prayer is based on the intersection as it acknowledges Jesus as the Christ sent by God to the world. Without being specific, this prayer asks for Jesus to intervene on behalf of the person making the prayer. The person is acknowledging that they cannot achieve their own enlightenment and salvation because of their separation from God. This prayer is powerful, short, and rhythmic.

This rhythmic aspect of a prayer can manifest commonly in the rocking of the body in a rhythm. The rocking motion is soothing to the human body and also keeps the body busy. When the body is busy, it often releases the mind from the brain's constant need to validate itself via inane commentary.

Hands of Prayer / Mudra

The mudra is the placing of the hands into a specific configuration to stimulate a mental state. It is uncommon for mudra to be used without some other accompanying body position. The classic Western hands pressed together at the palms, often held in front of the face in prayer, is a mudra. In Buddhism, the hands are placed palm to palm as a greeting. Both Eastern and Western forms of this mudra express devotion in different cultures and different religions. The hand position remains the same. The hand position stimulates a Pavlovian response. Over time and repetition, this position of hands signals the brain and the mind that it is time to turn attention from whatever was to what is now.

In the same way that a word from a close relative can signal an emotion—love, or maybe sadness—a mudra can be used to signal specific behaviors. A mudra is an external signal from the body to the mind to set the protocol in motion. Trained over time, the mudra of prayer hands can signal a quicker and deeper response from the brain and the mind.

Stained Glass Window / Mandala

The mandala is a picture, a visual symbol that opens a window onto a new dimension. There is no restriction on the materials with which a mandala is constructed. A mandala can be made of sand, for which the Tibetan Buddhist's are famous, or it may be made of glass like the rose window in the Basilica of Our Lady of Chartres in France. Here are two-line illustrations of a Tibetan sand mandala and the Rose Window of Chartres.

Tibetan Sand Mandala   **Chartres Rose Window**

The idea that the mandala serves as a road sign to help us access another dimension lies in the preparation and creation of the mandala. These icons are prepared with a protocol of prayers and the artist is often in a contemplative state during its creation. With a focus on the mandala and its creation, the human mind can begin to alter its orientation in the world. With this alteration, the brain waves shift to a different frequency, and the person can open up to the Divine and receive.

Contemplation

"Everyone of us is shadowed by an illusory person: a false self.

We are not very good at recognizing illusions, least of all the ones we cherish about ourselves. Contemplation is not and cannot be a function of this external self."

- *Thomas Merton*[30], *New Seeds of Contemplation*

Contemplation is the Christian tradition that involves a silent focus. Sometimes this is called "a gaze of faith" or some other set of words that illustrate this focus. Focusing on an icon can bring forth the particular target. A contemplation for the prayer of a mother's love might involve a picture of the Mother Mary, or a candle flame for the ineffable brightness of the Holy Spirit. These objects serve as a tool of focus so that the mind may be released into the realm of contemplation.

Using aids for contemplation is not exclusively a Christian practice. They are used in both the Zen and Buddhist paths, as well.

Contemplation can be split into two forms: Acquired Contemplation and Infused Contemplation.

Acquired Contemplation

Acquired contemplation places the influence of the human intellect as its core quality. There can be assistance from the Divine in respect to achievement, but the key focus is the human intellect. Acquired contemplation is a road gently rising from sea level to the gentle rolling hills of the nearby inland. It can be vulnerable to fantasy. The mind can choose a road that is not going in the correct direction. External assistance from a spiritual director, counselor, mentor, or another person with some expertise in this field will aid in keeping on the right course.

Acquired contemplation has a deliberate thought process at work. You plan on the way you look at an idea, object or thought and there might be some form of the scientific process involved.

Using the scientific process as a means of acquired contemplation method reads this way:

Scientific Method

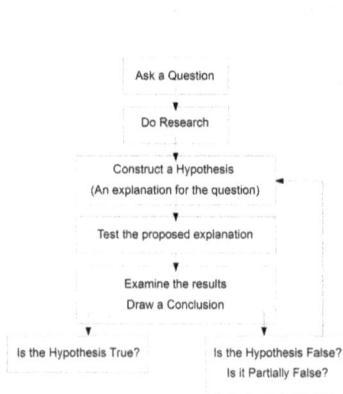

Ask a Question

Do Research

Construct a Hypothesis
(An explanation for the question)

Test the proposed explanation

Examine the results
Draw a Conclusion

Is the Hypothesis True?

Is the Hypothesis False?
Is it Partially False?

There are two views of the word "inspiration." One definition contains the idea of divine stimulus brought to a person, and the other definition is a human version that emphasizes influence over the intellect or emotions. One version is vertical in the action, the Divine version; the other version is lateral, the humanist version. The divine version is favored; however, there are attributes of acquired contemplation that are attributes of acquired discipline.

Acquired contemplation means that the person has put a deliberate thought process to work. There is deliberation in how you might look at an idea, object, or thought. There is often some form of the scientific process, at least until the process gets to the testing aspect of the scientific method. Some of the commonly listed physical benefits of acquired contemplation, as well as infused contemplation, are an increase in immunity and increased fertility. It is the author's supposition, and not medically proven, that the reasons for these two particular results are that the relaxed body is unified and feels safe. A relaxed body provides better coordination of the physical systems.

Brainwaves

There are four levels of brain activity: beta, alpha, theta, and delta. These four brainwaves are recorded by measuring the changing electrical impulses within the brain.

Beta waves range between 14 and 30 cycles per second. This beta state is the state of a person who is awake, alert, or excited. This is a state of somebody who is working and deeply focused, whether working at a desk or chopping wood.

Alpha waves vary from eight to thirteen cycles per second. This state is characterized by deep relaxation and passive awareness. It is sometimes described as a "focused non-focus" state.

Theta is a frequency that runs from four to seven cycles per second. Characteristics of this state are akin to a person who is drowsy, bordering on unconsciousness. You are in a theta state as you are falling asleep on the couch, but you're still able to understand the conversation that is going on around you.

Delta has the quality of a half a cycle to four cycles per second. If you are in delta state you are asleep, unconscious.

Brain Waves

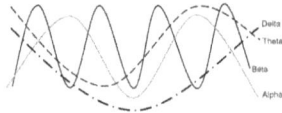

The ability to switch quickly from the beta state to the alpha state of mind is the realm of the mystic. It's also the realm of the elite athlete. The elite athlete, no matter their sport, is able to train their brain activity to take them into "The Zone," or what the mystic may call the "The Flow." In 1954, Roger Bannister, an Olympic runner from England, became the first man to break the four-minute mile. When he spoke about his mental state when running, Bannister said, "I'm no longer conscious of my movement. I discovered a new unity with nature. I had found a new source of power and beauty, a source I never dreamt existed."

This flow is a result of shifting brainwaves. Sometimes the mystical training is familial: perhaps an aunt supporting a child's intuition, to more disciplined, and organized methods found in monasteries, or traditional mentorships and tutelage.

Regardless of exercise and methods, the ability to move from one brainwave level to another as the situation may require is an important skill that all people along the mystical path possess. This can be a gift, a learned skill, or both.

The Illuminated Intellect

The word "illuminated" is intended to indicate that the human mind is in contact with the Divine, in some manner or form. A necessary characteristic of the illuminated intellect is a mind that is intellectually prepared for rigorous thought.

This is where the mind, of its own accord, can create a brilliant and positive Divine Voice. But the voice is that of the mind and is totally human. It is the act of an academically prepared mind that is in the presence of the Divine generating its own profound voice, a brilliant yet human voice.

The Formal Divine Voice

The formal Divine voice is not always received in prayer. Its purpose is very specific. This voice carries the instructions for direction or action in the quest for perfection and union with the Divine.

Substantial

These substantial experiences are heard in the soul and make impactful change instantly. These substantial acts are so profound, so deep, and so thoroughly that they are of the realm of God, not man. There is no room in this moment for human or demonic distortion.

Simplicity and Asceticism

SIMPLE GIFTS

'Tis the gift to be simple, 'tis the gift to be free,
'Tis the gift to come down where we ought to be,
And when we find ourselves in the place just right,
'Twill be in the valley of love and delight.
When true simplicity is gain'd,
To bow and to bend we shan't be asham'd,
To turn, turn will be our delight
'Till by turning, turning we come round right.
                                    - Elder Joseph Brackett, Jr[31].

One Thanksgiving in my early adulthood, my parents came over for holiday. My mother set out to diligently construct a Thanksgiving Day meal in my kitchen. As the day went on, her frustration increased as she discovered how little in the way of kitchen implements I had on hand. The very next day, she went out and bought me a couple of pans and some utensils. Shortly after that, my mother handed me a box that contained, forks, knives, spoons, and other items you would use for a table setting. "Your father wants you have these," she said as she handed them to me. "I told your dad you live pretty lean, but he still thought it was a good idea." It was a wonderful gift, thoughtful and insightful.

Two years later, I ran into the box of forks and knives, still unopened. I smiled, half because the utensils were a symbol of my parent's concern and love for me, and half because I knew that they didn't really understand what was taking place. I was practicing my version of minimalism and simplicity. A wonderful experience all the way around.

Eric Hoffer[32], the author of ten books including the classic, "The True Believer," was awarded the Presidential Medal of Freedom in 1983 for his body of work. Hoffer was a longshoreman who lived in a one-room apartment and didn't own a TV. Hoffer clearly lived a minimal life, yet he smoked cigars. Are Hoffer's cigars inconsistent with your vision of minimalism?

If you look at minimalism as giving and not taking, you will be very successful. Hoffer's minimal life brought him time, and clarity, focusing on Hoffer's cigar misses the true crux of the minimal existence.

The human mind works in this way: If a doctor tells you that you have a 10% chance of dying on the operating table, you will begin to measure your operation in that context. The mind begins to ramble with thoughts, "If I go into that operating room 10 times, I'm not coming out one of those times, and maybe this might be that one time." You'll have thoughts that measure the success of that operation by its failure rate. If the doctor says, "It's going to be a difficult operation, and it won't be without risk. But we have a very high success rate—90% of our patients go on to live the rest of their life, enjoying it with virtually no side effects."

See how your mind measures it differently? This is how minimalism should be viewed, as gaining the things that we value: clarity, cleanliness, and the lack of clutter. We gain time because we don't have to service items. We gain appreciation for the simplest and most creative ways tools can be used. One of the most valued benefits, yet often overlooked, is a lack of ambient frustration. A calmness arises from not needing to attend to many external items in our lives.

> *"Clothed in camel's hair, with a leather belt around his waist. He fed on locusts and wild honey" (Mk 1:6)*

This is how the Bible depicts John the Baptist, a popular ascetic. Asceticism is recognized by its lack of trappings. It is the act of removing.

Most often, the act of removing is centered on what might be called a richness, or affluence. But it goes deeper, severing the extras and what some might consider the essentials of life. There are many expressions of asceticism, and those expressions can take on levels that can be based on exaggerations and projections. The expression of asceticism can also last a lifetime or a short time, such as months or a year.

Asceticism, in its purest definition, is a lifestyle that deliberately sets aside certain aspects of life—sexual activity, drinking alcohol, intoxicants—to practice restraint in order to benefit the mind, body, and spirit.

The Desert Fathers moved into caves away from the general public. Later renunciants included monks that moved into monasteries. Many orders across cultures often shut themselves away from the rest of the world. This environment builds a deeply structured system. Each monk has a peer group that surrounds him twenty-four hours a day, every day of the year. With this peer review and a life anchored by prescriptive prayer, it becomes very difficult to deviate from the path. The ascetic, monastic lifestyle is very structured, much supported, and very deliberate.

Historical asceticism involves extreme acts as self-flagellation, the act of whipping one's self with a flagellum or a Roman whip. Christ was whipped with a flagellum prior to his crucifixion, and in emulation the act was picked up by ascetic Christianity and was used as a punishment for offenses. In some instances, flagellation was performed by a superior or with a specially designed flagellum by oneself. The mortification, or "putting the flesh to death" of the body, is not necessary and represents one of the most extreme forms of physical abuse in the name of religious experience.

In some instances, the body was considered to be a barrier to true illumination. As a result, it was not treated well. A form of mortification of the body included the lack of a nourishing diet. Given the context of the times, scarcity of food was a very serious matter, and diversity of food was not known like it is today. It wasn't a large step to simply move to a diet of water with the addition of some form of bread. Whatever was available locally was used to nourish the body, but in a reduced capacity. Although fasting and denial are traditionally part of the Christian experience, as in the season of Lent, it is simply not done in such an extreme manner as to place the health of the practitioner at risk. One only needs to look at the effect of anorexia on the human body to understand that this extreme form of denial is not healthy.

> *"Macarius, the Abbot said to Zacharias, the student, 'Tell me, what makes a monk?'*
>
> *He said, 'Isn't it wrong for you to be asking me?'*
>
> *Macarius said to him, 'I am sure I should ask you, Zacharias, my son. There is something that urges me to ask you.'*
>
> *Zacharias said to him, 'As far as I can tell, Abba, I think anyone who controls himself and makes himself*

*content with just what he needs and no more, is indeed
a monk.'"*

- *The Desert Fathers[33]: Sayings of the Early
Christian Monks by Benedicta Ward*

To live simply in the world, you needn't be an ascetic, but you may wish to audit certain aspects of your life. How much clothing do you have? Do you wear your entire wardrobe? Is the food you eat complex, rich, and exotic? What type of car do you drive? Do you desire the biggest, fastest, and best? The question is simply this: How much do you need to move through the world?

This is a decision to strike out on a trajectory to winnow the details of your external life down to a suitable level, where the very act of managing it is as simple and uncomplicated as possible. This type of change rarely comes overnight. The goal is not the minimalist lifestyle; this lifestyle comes because your focus is on your inner life.

It is a difficult task to achieve a balance living in this world while keeping your face turned towards the Divine. The difficulty comes from the constant interplay of diving into the world with its demands and focus, then diving into the Divine, and then re-entering the world again while awash in the delights of the godly. The goal is to use the experience of the Divine to enrich the life of the world and use the experience of the world to create a greater desire for God. This is the difficulty of the life of simplicity in the world.

Minimalism is the preferred path when attempting to live a mystical existence and still function in the world. Asceticism is often difficult while trying to live in the world.

Purgation

Purgation is an overarching action characteristic of the spiritual experience. It hovers above and through life.

Everybody on this journey hits moments of aridity, where is seems as nothing is happening and the Divine has retreated after a delightful and often powerful experience. Embrace the aridity and let it be. Don't look back, and don't look forward. "The Dark Night of the Soul" is a poem written by St. John of the Cross. This poem's title became a popular term to use during the time of aridity, but there is a distinct difference between aridity and The Dark Night of the Soul.

Aridity is just like the quote of Saint- Exupéry says: you see little, you hear little, yet something is present. It is elusive but it is not hiding. Turn towards it and it is not there. It moved, but again, it is still present. This is the time where you must simply put one foot in front of the other.

The Dark Night of the Soul is a temporary crisis and not one born out of the sadness that may be associated with the kind of depression that accompanies the loss of a loved one or a relationship. Although these may be an entry into the experience of the Dark Night of the Soul, the popular use of the phrase is not a reflection of the experience. This engrossment requires deep auditing as well as the assistance of a spiritual advisor.

Diabolical Assaults: When the Devil Comes A-calling

> *"I often laugh at Satan, and there is nothing that makes him so angry as when I attack him to his face, and tell him that through God I am more than a match for him."*
>
> *- Martin Luther*[35]

Much time is spent on the diabolical: the devil and demons. Demonic attacks make for great movies, television shows, and books. This form of entertainment can be so visceral that we focus a large amount of time on it. A movie about a person slowly opening up to the Divine is not very action-packed, so popular culture takes us on a demonic ride of thrills and threats to titillate our senses. While doing this, we turn an inordinate amount of focus to demons and the devil. This attention should be guarded against and not taken too seriously, simply because there are not demons behind every lamppost.

Thus, we mock cultures of history for their fear of the demonic. We call into question the less-than-enlightened behaviors of societies that do not take the leap into the modern world instead of questioning what has brought these behaviors into part of their culture.

Lisa and the Dark Man

Lisa said the entity appeared in her bedroom. It was taller than the average person, dark, and without clear edges. He spoke to her. This entity was frightening at first. But as it revealed portions of the future, and things that he said would happen came true, she began to believe that it spoke the truth. "It tells me it is ok to smoke and that I am different."

This entity first manifested after Lisa's divorce. Married at eighteen and divorced within a year, the line of trauma was a natural one to plumb, as it was an easy entrée for dark ones to exercise their intents.

As it turned out, Lisa's husband was involved in a satanic cult. Chalk it up to her young years, young love, lack of religious experience, and naiveté, she tacitly let things go. "It is just a social club, like bowling or something." Lisa rationalized her husband's behavior until it got bad.

Lisa went on, "You see, one girl from the group wanted my husband. She was serious and said to my face that she would get him, that she would take him away from me and make him hers. I took it seriously. I just did what I knew to do. I talked to my husband about what was said, and I kept as close an eye out as possible."

"The night we had the last fight, he blew up and left the house, got into the car, and blasted out of the driveway. Then the phone rang. It was her, the woman that said she would have my husband. She said, 'I said I told you I would have him,' and then she snickered."

The dark guy made it clear to Lisa that she didn't need a church or any of that kind of stuff. He said that she should go her own way because she was bright enough to do so. She realized that she could get help, she went and sought help from a person who could help her to battle the manifestation. It took some time, but with a little coaching in the use of a prayer she, Lisa was able to have God unfetter her of this dark man.

The Bible speaks clearly of demons:

> *Ephesians 6*
>
> *12 For we wrestle not against flesh and blood, but against principalities, against powers, against the rulers of the darkness of this world, against spiritual wickedness in high places.*
>
> *13 Wherefore take unto you the whole armor of God that ye may be able to withstand in the evil day and having done all, to stand.*

Every major religion speaks about demons or some form of sentient evil. For example, this evil can go by the name Jinn in Islam, and Suras in Hinduism.

In the book, *People of the Lie: The Hope for Healing Human Evil*, author M. Scott Peck addresses the idea of evil. He breaks it down into three categories:

- Illusory: That the idea of evil is not real. As an example, the Bahá'í Faith sees evil as a manifestation of base human traits that manifest when a person chooses to turn away from God.

- Integrated dualism: Since God gave us free will with the ability to choose, we also have the ability of choosing evil. This is the most common explanation used for the question, "Why is there evil in the world?"
- Diabolical Dualism: This is expressed by Lucifer as a purposeful and willful attack on God and his creation.

Pushback

Demons will fight for what they believe to be theirs. This can be described as a metaphysical shove or a pushback. This can manifest in many ways as attacks on your body, processions, or institutions. These attacks can be used to create pressure on you. The Book of Job, in the Bible, is an example of the potential for attacks. A condensed version of the Book of Job sounds like this:

God says, "Job is a great child of mine. He loves me."

The devil says, "Sure, he has everything, but what if he didn't? I'll bet you that he will renounce you if I take it all."

And the rest of the story tells you the pain that the devil lays on Job, who comes close, but never renounces God.

Of course, this is a very simplistic version of the Book of Job, but it is used in this way to make a point. When you turn your face to God and begin the mystical path, you become a target for demons.

Here's another way to look at this journey and how you are perceived by the dark entities: demons are headhunters that are only interested in placing your head on a stake outside their hut. The more you seek, the more valuable your head becomes to them. The best way to ensure that you fail is to ensure that you never really get started, to nip it in the bud. The stronger your walk on the path, the stronger the pushback from the darkness. If you are on the mystical path, you may experience such an intrusion.

These dark entities deal in legalities. For instance, if a child asks you for a lollipop, and you say, "No, it's too close to dinner time," you may find that same child eating a piece of chocolate a few moments later. You admonish the child by saying, "I told you that you couldn't have candy. It was too close to dinner!" And the child says, "No you told me I couldn't have a lollipop. This chocolate." A shrewd child and the demonic realms are similar in this way.

The ultimate goal of every demonic entity is the destruction of God's creation. The formula is very simple: make you destroy yourself, or destroy others, or destroy others and yourself. This is the greatest form of mockery: to have God's creation turned inward bent on its own destruction.

We can never know God in totality; however, the beginning of this journey that never ends is to counter what the demonic desire is for you, as we already discussed. Demons want to be sure that you will not complete your journey to meet the Divine. And they will do just about anything to prevent you from reaching this goal.

Always apply Occam's razor to anything transpiring around you. William of Occam was a Franciscan friar from the 1200s that created a simple method of deducing what is happing around you. A simple translation of Occam's razor is, when you are given multiple possible explanations for a problem the simplest explanation is the most likely.

To immediately assume that something is demonic because actions resulted that seem out of the norm is not the best course of action. Remain circumspect during these times. The guidance of a trusted spiritual counselor can help you to keep steadfast progress on the correct metaphorical road.

There are two forms of demonic assault: internal and external:

- Internal assaults can include harassment of your mental and physical acuity. These attacks and can manifest as, but are not limited to, anything from aches and pains to pounding headaches. Such maladies can be difficult to diagnose. However, it is important that you seek medical attention. Always avail yourself of every reasonable diagnosis and remedy that medicine has to offer.

- External assaults can be found in bureaucracies and agencies because they are easily manipulated. Bureaucracies can lose paperwork, claim no receipt of payments, and to create moments of consternation.

Focusing your anger at demons for what they've done plays directly into their hands. Here is the most simple and expeditious manner to deal with them: state that they do not have a claim to you and that whatever claim they believe they have is no longer in existence. Also, declare that you are requesting Christ to intervene on your behalf to have this claim removed. It is also important that you bless them with a true and thoughtful heart. This action shines the light of the creator on them, and it is difficult for them to bear. If you continue to have manifestations or assaults, it is important that you contact a person who can assist you in the analysis and the remediation of the problem.

Understand that these situations are real and significant. They should be dealt with in a manner that reflects the gravity of their situation.

The Occult

The word occult is highly charged in our world. It refers to any system that claims to have a use or special knowledge of the supernatural, their powers, or their personalities. The root of this word is from the Latin word Occulere, which means "to hide from view." In the Western world, when we hear the word occult, we tend to think of witches and warlocks, magical spells, and insidious behaviors. In some manifestations, these opinions are true. However, this is a caricature of these experiences, and thus, it is assumed that they should not be treated seriously. This is a great deception.

The occult works. It is real. Sometimes, while chasing the mystical experience, people seek out shortcuts: promises of higher experience with less effort or with some magical means to a position of enlightenment, special powers, considerations, or position. Understand this: the path is narrow, and dalliances with the occult will result in a serious misstep on your journey.

Do not fear the occult, but be respectful of it, in the same way that one would be respectful of a dog that has a history of biting. Do not place yourself in situations that you can be taken advantage of mentally, physically, or spiritually.

If it is the desire of the reader to pursue more information, do so with the deepest caution and with the knowledge you are placing much at risk.

Vision

*"Children are remarkable for their intelligence and ardor,
for their curiosity, their intolerance of shams, the clarity
and ruthlessness of their vision."*

- Aldous Huxley[36]

Words are utterances that create symbols in our mind.
When you hear the word "tree," you don't think of the
letters T-R-E-E. You think of a symbol of a tree. If you
grew up in the Pacific Northwest of the United States,
the symbol of the tree in your mind might be a cedar
tree. If you grew up in Southern California, the word
might remind you of a palm tree. In the Deep South,
you might think of a willow tree. The symbols that are
in our minds are triggered by the words. The words are a
tertiary example of the truth. And the truth is hidden by
a symbol.

The language of the human mind is symbolic. Thus,
visions that speak in symbols are very powerful. Symbols
are an entire study unto themselves. There are secular,
religious, sacred, and profane symbols. All are able to
communicate quickly and across multiple cultures.

When you see a red circle with a line through it, it means
"No." It can also mean "don't enter," or it can mean
almost anything in a negative. Just by putting a secondary

symbol inside the red cross-hatched circle, the symbol becomes a no parking sign, or it becomes a no smoking symbol. Therefore, the idea that the Divine communicates in symbols, in lieu of words, comes from the simplicity of this communication. It needs little translation.

Further, there are certain universal aspects of human existence that are uniform. For example, a smile can reach across cultures as a form physical communication. If you smile in France, it means the same thing as it does in Russia, Canada, and Japan. Another symbol that crosses cultures without explanation is the pose of standing with your hands at waist level and with open palms. This is a non-threatening, welcoming image. It says by default, "I have no weapons, and you are welcome." Little translation is needed and much is communicated.

If you should have a vision of The Mother Mary, and she appears smiling with her arms open, this becomes a symbol of a Mother's love. This is the female energy expressing its uniqueness for the purpose of conveying the love that only a mother has. Add a white sparkling robe, and you have some areas of flexibility in translation. In one culture, the white may be a representation of purity, and in another, it may represent the passing from this world to another.

Translation is best left to the individual who experiences the vision and not to a community of translators. If there is some confusion with your vision, a person with more experience—a trusted advisor, religious leader, or somebody who has had these experiences—can be of assistance.

Non-universal, specific symbols are very personal to the one having the experience. In the same way that we discussed the differences in the symbolic variances with trees, context becomes important. Cultural differences are present in visions and will appear according to how they can best reach the person having the experience. The goal of the Divine is to communicate a message and not have the messenger get in the way of the message. If you are expecting to receive a package, and a person wearing a tutu delivers the package, no matter the contents of the package and your anticipation of its arrival, you will focus on the delivery person's dress. Your focus will turn away from the contents of the package and your anticipation of its arrival.

Angels are a great example of how we interpret visions personally. They can appear fearsome in some instances, and yet they can also bring comfort. It all depends upon the message and need.

Visions are often the result of a premeditated request on your behalf. We set out and cast our minds through prayer and attention to bring about some type of experience. The vision is requested. This can happen during prayer, meditation, contemplation, or another form of altered state. Visions do not necessarily materialize at the instance of a request. They may appear after much preparation at an unexpected time, or even in a dream. The request was heard and the moment was set aside in our world, until the proper time when you are receptive and the right context presents itself.

Conclusion

This book is only a basic overview of the mystical experience. So by its nature, it is incomplete. It is the author's hope that this book will provide the basic structure for your path. Look at it as the pegs on walls of the entryway to your home. They are there for your coats so that you can enter and be comfortable. There are many, many manuscripts, books, and lessons that are deeper and more profound than the overview that is present here. Seek the deeper lessons, find them, learn them, and practice them.

Blessings and peace be with you.

Bibliography

Christian Gaser, G. S. (8 October 2003). Brain Structures Differ between Musicians and Non-Musicians. *The Journal of Neuroscience*.

Dr. Andrew Newberg, M. M. (2010). *How God Changes Your Brain: Breakthrough Findings from a Leading Neuroscientist*. Ballantine Books.

Jung, C. (1955). *Modern man in search of the soul*. Harcourt Harvest.

Scaramelli, G. (2005). *Scaramelli, G.B. A Handbook of Mystical Theology*. Berwick, Maine: Ibis.

Sun Sentinel, The. August 17, 2001, *Mom: God Told Me To Kill My Baby*, Gabriel Margasak.

Ward, Benedicta. (2003). *Sayings of the Early Christian Monks*: Penguin Classics

Endnotes

1   Pierre Teilhard de Chardin (1881 – 1955) was philosopher and author as well as a member of The Society of Jesus, The Jesuits. Chardin was also a paleontologist and geologist. He wrote The Phenomenon of Man

2   Thomas à Kempis (1380-1471) was a German priest who was believed to be the most likely author of The Imitation of Christ.

3   Brother Lawrence of the Resurrection (1614 – 1691) was a lay brother in a Paris monastery of the Carmelite order. He wrote The Practice of the Presence of God, which was complied from his works after his death.

4   St. Anthony of the Desert (251-356) is considered the father of all Christian monks, although he was not the first Christian monk. Anthony is known for giving away his inheritance and retreating to the Egyptian desert.

5   Lao Tzu (6th Century BC) was a Chinese philosopher who authored the Tao Te Ching, considered to be a fundamental text of Taoism.

6   Johann Wolfgang von Goethe (1749- 1832) was a German writer of poetry who also engaged in science, art, and statesmanship. His most famous work may be the play Faust, considered to be one of the greatest works of German literature.

7   Ambrose Gwinnett Bierce (1842-1914]) was an

American short story writer. His works include An Occurrence at Owl Creek Bridge, and The Devil's Dictionary.

8   Sir Winston Leonard Spencer-Churchill (1874 –1965) was the Prime Minister of the United Kingdom from 1940 to 1945 and again from 1951-1955. He is considered one of the greatest leaders of the 20th century.

9   James Thomas Anthony "Jim" Valvano (1946 – 1993), who went by the nickname "Jimmy V," was an American college basketball coach for North Carolina State University who gave a noted speech about life and cancer, and won the 1983 National Championship.

10   The Byrds were a rock band that began in Los Angeles, California in 1964, and had their first charting single with the Pete Seeger-penned, Turn, Turn, Turn, based on Chapter 3 of the Book of Ecclesiastes.

11   Bull Durham was a 1988 movie about a hapless minor league baseball team, starring Kevin Costner, Susan Sarandon, and Tim Robbins.

12   Donald John Trump, Sr., (1946 -) began his business empire in real estate. He is the president of the Trump Organization, and the several other investments and financial interests.

13   Mahatma Gandhi, Mohandas Karamchand Gandhi (1869-1948) was a leader of the Indian independence movement opposing British rule. Gandhi was a proponent of non-violent resistance.

14   Bertrand Arthur William Russell (1872 – 1970) was a British political anti-war activist, social commentator, and

philosopher. He is considered to be one to the founders of analytic philosophy.

15   Epictetus, (55 − 135) was a Greek philosopher of the Stoic school. He was born a slave in what is modern day Turkey and died in northern Greece. He believed people are responsible for their own actions and can control their own behaviors via discipline.

16   Stephen Richards Covey, (1932-2012) was the Author and creator of The Seven Habits of Highly Effective People. He was also a businessman and public speaker.

17   Leo Tolstoy, (1828 − 1910) also known as, Count Lev Nikolayevich Tolstoy, was a Russian writer, philosopher and political thinker who is famous for the novels, War and Peace and Anna Karenina, among others.

18   Abraham Harold Maslow, (1908 − 1970) was an American psychologist who created Maslow's hierarchy of needs, a theory of mental health based on fulfilling human needs in sequence, building on each with the aim of self actualization.

19   Robert Frost (1874 − 1963) was an American poet whose work often depicted rural American life.

20   Aristotle (384–322 BC) was a Greek philosopher and scientist as well as a teacher of Alexander the Great. Through his work, he established ways of thinking that are present to this day.

21   Bertrand Arthur William Russell, (see end note xiv)

22   Fulton John Sheen (1895-1979) was a Bishop in the Roman Catholic Church who was a popular radio and television personality.

23   Mark Twain was the pen name for Samuel Langhorne Clemens, (1835-1910) an American author and humorist. He wrote The Adventures of Tom Sawyer and The Adventures of Huckleberry Finn.

24   Helen Adams Keller (1880 – 1968) was an American lecturer, political activist, and author. The film, The Miracle Worker, depicts her early life.

25   Damian Lewis (1971-) was an Emmy and Golden Globe winning English actor and producer.

26   Beverly Sills (1929 – 2007) was an American opera singer.

27   Billie Holiday (born Eleanora Fagan; 1915 –1959) was an American jazz singer. She was famous for her phrasing and tempo.

28   Frank Sinatra (Francis Albert "*Frank*" *Sinatra* 1915 – 1998) was a multi-talented American singer, actor, director, film producer, and conductor whose career spanned five decades.

29   Ralph Waldo Emerson (1803-1882) was an American poet, essayist, and lecturer who in the 19th century led the Transcendentalist movement.

30   Thomas Merton, *Order of Cistercians of the Strict Observance*, O.C.S.O. (1915 – 1968) was a Trappist monk of the

Abbey of Gethsemani in Kentucky and an American Catholic writer.

31   Elder Joseph Brackett, Jr. (1797 - 1882) was a Shaker Elder who penned the song, "Simple Gifts." He was born, lived, and died in the state of Maine.

32   Eric Hoffer (1902-1983) was an American philosopher who addressed moral and social ideas.

33   The Desert Fathers were Christian hermits, ascetics, and monks who lived in the desert of Egypt beginning around the third century AD.

34   Antoine de Saint-Exupéry (1900 – 1944) was a French aristocrat, writer, poet, and aviator. He wrote The Little Prince (Le Petit Prince.)

35   Martin Luther, Order of Saint Augustine, (OSA) (1483 – 1546) was a German monk, Catholic priest, Professor of theology and essential figure of the 16th century movement in the Protestant Reformation.

36   Aldous Leonard Huxley (1894 –1963) was an English writer best known for his dystopian novel, Brave New World, set London.

Kris has worked as a bartender, construction worker, disc jockey, political and public affairs consultant, and has been on legislative and political staffs at the state and federal levels. Currently, Kris is the head instructor and owner of West Seattle Karate Academy. Kris started practicing the martial arts at the age of fifteen. Over the years, he has earned black belt rankings in three styles, Goju-Ryu karate, taekwondo, and judo, in which he has competed in senior nationals and international tournaments. Kris is also a member of the Order of St. Francis, a contemporary expression of Franciscan tradition within the Anglican Communion. His books focus on personal growth and awareness through internal and external training. Kris makes his home in the Seattle metropolitan area of Washington State.